How To Know When God Speaks

by

Helen Hosier

Except where otherwise indicated, all Scripture quotations in this book are taken from the King James Version of the Bible.

Verses marked AMP are taken either from The Amplified Old Testament, Copyright © 1962 and 1964 by Zondervan Publishing House, or from The Amplified New Testament, Copyright © 1954 and 1958 by The Lockman Foundation. Used by permission.

Verses marked NASB are taken from The New American Standard Bible, © The Lockman Foundation 1960, 1962, 1963, 1968, 1971, 1972, 1973, 1975. Used by permission.

Verses marked NKJB are taken from The New King James Bible, Copyright © 1979 by Thomas Nelson, Inc. Publishers. Used by permission.

Verses marked RSV are taken from The Revised Standard Version of the Bible, Copyright 1946 and 1952 by the Division of Christian Education of the National Council of the Churches of Christ in the United States of America. Used by permission.

Verses marked TLB are taken from The Living Bible, Copyright 1971 by Tyndale House Publishers. Used by permission.

HOW TO KNOW WHEN GOD SPEAKS

Copyright © 1980 by Helen Kooiman Hosier

Published by Harvest House Publishers
Irvine, California 92714
Library of Congress Catalog Card Number 79-84721
ISBN 0-89081-197-0

Printed in the United States of America.

Speak, Lord, in the stillness,
While I wait on Thee;
Hushed my hear to listen
In expectancy.

Speak, O blessed Master,
In this quiet hour;
Let me see Thy face, Lord,
Feel Thy touch of power.

For the words Thou speakest,
They are life indeed;
Living bread from Heaven,
Now my spirit feed!

Speak, Thy Servant heareth!
Be not silent, Lord;
Waits my soul upon Thee
For the quickening word!
—Author Unknown

Acknowledgments

I am a gleaner, gathering up some of the choicest morsels that have come to my attention in order to share them with you. I acknowledge with gratitude the inspiration and help I have received over the years from these writers. Books are among the great counselors that God has given to us.

I acknowledge too the responses to my requests to friends to share their insights and experiences. What you read here is the result of putting it all together.

I am especially indebted to Bob Hawkins, who gently prodded me on to completion and caught the vision of the need for a book addressing itself to this subject.

My husband and son as usual have had to give me up on many evenings and weekends. For their thoughtfulness and concern I feel blessed.

Affectionately I dedicate this to my children and grandchildren with the prayer that it will help them and the reader to know that God does speak, He does listen to our prayers, and He does answer.

Helen Kooiman Hosier
June 1980

Other Books by Helen Kooiman Hosier

JOYFULLY EXPECTANT: Meditations Before
   Baby Comes
CAMEOS: Women Fashioned by God
SUICIDE: A Cry for Help
THE OTHER SIDE OF DIVORCE
THE CARING JESUS
PROFILES: People Who Are Helping to Change
   the World
STRUCK BY LIGHTNING, THEN BY LOVE (with
   Wilma Stanchfield)
BETTER THAN I WAS (with Frances Kelley)
CORONARY? CANCER? GOD'S ANSWER:
   PREVENT IT! (with Dr. Richard Brennan)
NEVER SAY NEVER TO GOD (with
   Nell Maxwell)
IT FEELS GOOD TO FORGIVE

Contents

CHAPTER
1

God Or Your Imagination?

When we listen to God, then people will listen to us. —E. Stanley Jones

Chapter 1

"EITHER he's got an overworked imagination, or he's in communication with a different God from the God I know and the God revealed in the Bible," I said to my husband with a groan. It wasn't the first time I had experienced that kind of reaction after hearing someone say, "God told me. . . ."

God gets blamed for many things that are really not His doing at all. We also attribute His leading to things we do or say when we haven't waited for His direction. Sometimes we wait and wait but still aren't sure when, where, or if God is leading. I'm sure God gets credit for things He would just as soon not be given credit for! How easy it is to say, "God told me." I can't help wondering how many people have been turned off and turned away from seeking God's leading by our easy "God told me."

I wonder if we're hearing what God is saying—or are we proceeding full steam ahead with what we intended to do all along? We get ourselves off the hook by our praying, and we mentally pat ourselves on the back by saying to ourselves, "There, I've committed it to God in prayer."

But have we really sought His leading, or have we just told Him what we wanted, so that later on we can say, "God told me." What we really wanted was His *approval*, not His *guidance* and certainly not a "No" when we wanted a "Yes"! "It's not for you to know" would throw all our plans off-kilter.

I have often asked the question, "How do you know God is speaking? How can you be sure it's God and not your imagination? Is it wishful thinking, or is it really God talking? And when He talks, how does He talk to you?"

The answers I've gotten have proven both interesting and helpful. What you read in this book is the result of long hours of research and reading, sorting out my own thoughts and reactions, sifting through memories, and reading and rereading many letters in answer to my questions about God's leading.

Recently friends have said to me, "What are you writing now?" I have responded by saying, "Would it surprise you if I told you I'm trying to tackle the subject of how you know when God is speaking?" The response is inevitably the same: everyone is bothered by the flippant way so many people say, "God told me," and then relate an incident that leaves you wondering if they are talking about the same God you have come to know!

"The Lord told me" or "The Lord revealed to me" or "God said" or "God led me"—how often we hear those words or something similar! We sometimes say them ourselves. But what are we actually saying?

A contributing editor to a Christian journal wrote a tongue-in-cheek editorial that caught my eye. His timely comments added fuel to the fire that was burning in my heart.

> *I guess I'm a Christian of little faith. Students come to me from time to time, flinty of eye, claiming that God has led them to this or that. One told me God had led him to believe that his Word was sufficient, and it was up to me to convince him that the text in my literature course was worth reading . . .*
>
> *Youth, of course, will be swerved. But lately I've heard from mature people whom I respect [that they have] an easy access to God's leading that causes me to wonder. How do we know that it's God, not Satan, whose map we follow? . . .*
>
> *I like to ask God to lead me, too. I'd be happy if His wisdom would get around to recognizing the raise and promotion I could use . . . .*[1]

Writer Joe Bayly maintains that one of the most serious concerns among students today relates to guidance. "Holiness may have been the passion of another generation's young men and women . . . but not today. Today the theme is getting to know the will of God."[2]

This concern is also shared by most serious adult Christians today. Students aren't the only ones who are seeking to understand God's will. Many are thinking (if not verbalizing) the question, "How do you know when God speaks?"

In recent years my husband and I have had our lives greatly enriched by the friendship of John and Goldia Mills. I can always count on them for wise counsel. When I read Proverbs 27:17 I think of these friends: "Iron sharpens iron; so one man sharpens another" (NASB). They motivate me to think more creatively, and are quick to affirm me when they sense this is what I need.

John Mills' letter (in answer to my question) stated:

I hope you have a thick skin, and are a good swimmer . . . . You are jumping into a controversial subject, to be sure. There's an awful price to pay for not conforming.

How does God speak to us today, or doesn't He speak at all? There's a world of difference between the creeds of the church and the dogma we preach. There's an even greater gulf between what we preach and what we practice.

Most of us have said for a long time that God speaks through the Scriptures. But there are others who are always looking for a word from the Lord for every situation, beginning with which shoe to put on first in the morning!

Hearing God speak and knowing the will of God are one and the same thing. Most of us are looking for a blueprint for our lives; God most often leads one day at a time.

Legalism says that only those things expressly approved are permitted to us. I believe that all things not expressly forbidden are usually acceptable to God. I believe, for instance, that God wants me to enjoy a good meal in a beautiful place provided I'm not squandering my living in expensive places all the time, or I'm not running from something I know God wants more at that time (providing I'm not going against God's written Word).

The same would be true of work, recreation, or worship. All are equally spiritual. In fact, fullness of the Spirit always issues in family living, in right relations where we work, and how we spend and give our money.

The person who is living short of God's will for this moment would not recognize God if He spoke; indeed, they cannot hear because they will not recognize God's voice. As long as I am living in stubborn disobedience, I cannot hear God when He speaks. I miss the meaning of His words . . . .

I have never heard an audible voice, but two or three times I have heard as clearly as though God had spoken audibly to me. Each time occurred when I was having a difference with God. Each time He came out clearly the Victor. Jesus is Lord.

Most often He simply gives a settled abiding certainty deep within me concerning His will for me. How it comes is difficult to say. In most cases it would be an easy matter to explain His will away. We need to always be sensitive and expectant concerning God's leading.

Usually Scripture is involved, but seldom to the exclusion of other means of leading. Many of our friends emphasize confirmation; I feel that they give this undue emphasis. Yet this is a valid way of seeking God's will. Counsel of godly men is a means, as are open and closed doors. Seldom have I ever had any certainty in *such matters from any one or two of these means alone.*

We need to seek and be open to every means of God's "speaking," but always we need to return to Scripture and the leadership of the Holy Spirit to prove or disprove His leadership.

How can a person know when God is talking? In the final analysis, I have to get my answers from the Scriptures: "The spiritual man makes judgments about all things, but he himself is not subject to any man's judgment: 'For who has known the mind of the Lord, that he may instruct him?' But we have the mind of Christ" (1 Corinthians 2:15,16 NIV).

There have been times when I have heard someone say that God revealed something to him (or her) and I have actually been embarrassed for the Lord's sake. On such occasions I've wanted to flee the room (auditorium, church, luncheon, or whatever). From what I have been able to gather, there are many of you who feel the same way.

What then can we say about making sure we are hearing God's voice? No longer do we have the kind of dramatic encounters with God that Adam, Moses, Abraham, Noah, Gideon, and many of the other Old Testament personalities had. (For that matter, the same is true of the New Testament people as well.) Have you heard of anyone bumping into a burning bush lately or hearing an audible voice, as Adam experienced in the Garden encounter? When we were undecided about a move some years ago, God didn't boom out and tell us to head for Houston. Come to think of it, Abraham's exodus from Ur of the Chaldees had a lot more certainty about it than some moves some of us have had to make in our lifetime!

One of my friends took exception to my statement that I had never heard God speak audibly, nor did I know anyone who had. She wrote:

> I think you are not reading the right books or material when you say, "I haven't heard of anyone hearing an audible voice [today]," because it's all around you.
>
> Someone has just told me of an experience that happened several years ago when she had to make a trip of several miles in the rain to keep an engagement she had made against her better judgment. As she was dressing an audible voice said, "You will never make it!" Sure enough, on her way on the freeway, in order to avoid a car stalled ahead of her, she applied her brakes, skidded and crashed into a fence, wrecking the front of her car and losing consciousness.

My friend who wrote of this incident also told of reading an article in a Christian magazine about a mother who was standing at the kitchen sink washing dishes. She heard an audible voice say, "You must pray." She knew there was no one in the house with her, but the voice was so clear that she turned about to seek its source, only to find no one. She felt it must be the Lord. The article went on to describe the woman's reaction as she, in effect, said to the Lord, "I don't know what it is I am to pray about, Lord, but whoever it is that needs my prayer, I ask that you be with them; help them and sustain them."

Later this mother was to learn that her only son was coming down a mountain road from his logging job with a heavy motor in the back seat of his car. A tire blew out and he veered to the edge of the road. His one thought as the car started over the embankment was that if the motor was thrown forward it could kill him. At that moment the door beside him flew open and he was thrown clear. At that same moment the motor came hurtling past the spot where he had been sitting and crashed through the windshield. Later on, at home with his mother, they compared notes. The warning to the mother to pray had come just at the time this happened.

My friend's letter continued:

> *I too have "heard" the Lord speak to me, but not with an audible voice. The words seemed to go through my consciousness something like a telepathic message, but there was no mistaking the fact that the Lord was speaking.*

Here is the crux of the matter, and here is where we need to make ourselves plainly understood. Especially does this need exist when we are trying to communicate with those who may not understand our terminology. Precisely at this point we turn many people away from experiencing for themselves this vital kind of relationship with their Maker.

I do not question the experiences related to me. These were individuals who claimed to have heard God speak audibly. I have talked to dozens of people who walk with the Lord. Daily they seek His guidance for their lives, and they live in an exemplary manner before Him and the world. But not one of them has heard God speak audibly. So when I say that I haven't heard or known anyone who has had an experience similar to that of Adam as he walked in the Garden of Eden, or to that of Moses alone on the backside of the desert as he heard God calling to him from out of the bush (Exodus 3:4), what am I saying?

My friend's criticism was well-meant, and I took it in the manner in which it was intended, but it does point up the need to address ourselves to the question, "How do you know when God speaks?"

We are saying it; what are we meaning? What are others hearing? Are they looking at us and thinking, "If she's meaning what I think she's saying, then there must be something wrong with me because I sure don't hear God talking!"

E. Stanley Jones, in addressing himself to this problem, points out that he believes the dictation method of guidance is out—the method which dictates what we are to do for the day. God gave much of that kind of direction as recorded in Old Testament history, but as most theologians and serious Bible students point out, as people become spiritualized more and more (come into a realization of what the Apostle Paul talks about in 1 Corinthians 2), the guidance becomes inner. The inner nature is tuned to listen to God, to hear the divine whisper within.

There is no denying that wherever we look in the Old Testament we find "And God said . . . ." Did God actually verbalize out loud to these people? And if He did, why doesn't He do that today? Or is He doing it, and do you wonder why you aren't getting some of those messages?

John Mills points out that guidance in the Old Testament was often the black and the white stone, the long and the short broom straws divinely controlled. The last account of this is in the New Testament choice of a replacement for Judas (Acts 1:24-26). Mills asks the question, "Was this misguided, or did God fail to follow through?" The answer to that question is not simple. One must remember the Hebrew culture. Casting lots was a very respectable able way of determining a course of action. Perhaps the disciples were remembering the Old Testament proverb, "The lot is cast into the lap, but the whole disposing thereof is of the Lord" (Proverbs 16:33).

It would appear that the disciples were having the same problem as we have today—how do you know when God is speaking? There is variance of opinion as to whether the disciples in this instance were doing the right thing. Preceding verses assure us, however, that the disciples applied to God by prayer for direction, knowing Him as "the Searcher of hearts" (Acts 1:24). Furthermore, the two men selected were already known to be Christ's attendants. Matthew Henry states that casting of lots in this way is "lawful to be used for determining matters not otherwise determinable, provided it be done in a solemn religious manner, and with prayer, the prayer of faith."

After Pentecost and the coming of the Holy Spirit, there is the promise of the Holy Spirit dwelling in believers. He is the power of the church. We no longer read of black and white stones and casting of lots. Direction for the believer is directly related to the working of the Holy Spirit in one's life.

But the matter of hearing God speak can become perplexing and upsetting to those who feel they are being bypassed. Why did God choose to talk to some and not others? Surely He is not a God of exclusivity—including some at whim and excluding others. Haven't we all been created by the same reasonable God?

Does our questioning imply doubt or cynicism about God's fairness? For some people it may seem to imply doubt about His existence.

No, I am not doubting that God has spoken in times past and that He speaks today. It is God Himself who has gifted us with thought patterns that seek to know Him better; and stretching out our thinking we are not being cynical. Our capacity for knowing can become infinitely richer as we bring these questions under the scrutiny of what God has revealed in the Bible. As we look at the experiences of some of God's saints and of our contemporaries, and then think back on our own experiences, we should be able to come up with the right answers to these and other questions.

To be sure, this is a mind-stretching exercise, but a challenging one. Honest doubts as to whether we are hearing God's voice are always acceptable when our hearts are open before God and we truly want to make sure that it is *God* we are hearing rather than our own imaginations or the voice of the tempter.

CHAPTER
2

Trust And Obey

Before one can play any game he must know the rules, and certainly this is equally true about our living for Christ—we must be conversant with the rule book of life—the Bible.
—H. Gwynn Vaughn

CHAPTER 2

IN ORDER to recognize God's nudging, we have to know the Father. For as long as I can remember, I have been a God-conscious person. This God-consciousness was nurtured by my mother. (My father died five months before I was born.) There was never any doubt in my mind as a child that God and my mother had some kind of communication going. If a child is to come into an understanding of the reality of God's being, what better place to recognize this than in one's mother's life? I knew that she talked to God through prayer, and I sensed that He talked back to her somehow. I began to grasp the idea that God speaks to us.

I was 20 years old before I more fully understood that God's voice comes to us in many ways, but that one specific way we hear Him speak is through His Word to us. Mother had always insisted that we memorize Bible verses. I rebelled as a child and could only regard it as a tiresome ordeal to be endured. Life seemed to be one long "catechism session" of learning Bible verses. But as a young woman, the Bible verses that I had learned as a child came into my thinking at a crucial time, and they changed the direction of my life. This was God speaking to me. It was His Word (written to be sure) that I was hearing (remembering).

In researching and writing one of my books, I came across an old Jewish proverb which says, "God could not be everywhere, and so he made mothers." I think you will agree that this is as fine a tribute as has ever been written about the influence of godly mothers. We begin as infants, develop into children, become teenagers, and finally emerge as men and women. But what happens in between is all-important in shaping our destinies.

It has been my privilege to interview and spend time with the mothers of some of this century's most well-known Christian men. One of the things these men shared in common was mothers who made them memorize Bible verses. Morrow Graham, the mother of Billy Graham, spoke to me of Deuteronomy 6:4-7. "If this were practiced by parents, we would see far less unrest and problems in the country. The entire sixth chapter speaks to me of God-given home life and was most important in my life in bringing up our children."

This was God speaking to Mrs. Graham, telling her how to raise her children. What does this passage say?

> Hear . . . . The Lord our God is one Lord. Thou shalt love the Lord thy God with all thy heart, and with all thy soul, and with all thy might. And these words, which I command thee this day, shall be in thy heart; and thou shalt teach them diligently unto thy children, and shalt talk of them when thou sittest in thy house, and when thou walkest by the way, and when thou liest down, and when thou risest up.

I think we would have to say that Morrow Graham got the message that God intended, and that we have seen evidence of that in the life of her world-famous and much-respected son.

A dependence on God emerges as we begin to practice consciously sensing His presence, recognizing that He is speaking from the Bible. Then we become responsive to His nudges in other ways.

Certainly one of the ways that God has always communicated His will to individuals is through circumstances. More than one person has related this to me. It took a heartbreaking experience that devastated me and sent me into an emotional tailspin to make me realize that God was nudging me, telling me that now was the time to write this book.

The details of what happened are not important, and I don't want to hurt others who were involved. Suffice to say that the evening it happened I wept until I thought surely there could be no more tears where these were coming from. My heart was broken and I went to bed sobbing. I finally fell asleep. Tears, I am convinced, are God's tranquilizer. My husband and I had prayed together, and I knew in my heart that there was a reason for what had happened and that God was hearing our prayers, and that He saw my crushed spirit.

During the night I had a dream. I awoke in the morning and the dream was still vivid. My husband was shaving when I awoke and told him, "I had a dream last night. It was the most unusual dream, and I've got to tell you about it."

"No," he said, "you don't need to tell me about it. I already know you were dreaming."

I was surprised. "You know I had a dream?"

"Yes, you had a dream and you were laughing. You laughed and laughed. I almost woke you up, but then I listened, and it was beautiful laughter. You were so happy, and the laughter was joyous. I've never heard you laugh so happily."

Now I was really surprised. My husband had confirmed my dream and I hadn't even told him what had happened in that dream.

How does God communicate with us? How did He communicate to some of the men and women of the Bible? One of the ways in which He communicated was through dreams and visions. There are many Christians today who shy away from a recognition of the fact that God can still come to us in this way. Why do so many people back away from this as fact? Perhaps the answer lies in the abuse to which dreams and visions have been subjected. Some people *do* have vivid imaginations, and they let their imaginations get out of hand.

A look at the Bible reveals that God gave a vision to the Apostle John as he was alone and exiled on the Island of Patmos. He was told, "Write down what you have just seen, and what will soon be shown to you."[1]

The Apostle Paul was no stranger to dreams and visions. Because he heeded a vision one night in Troas, Paul and Silas and Timothy went westward to Europe instead of going to the provinces of Asia Minor, toward the east. "There stood a man of Macedonia . . . saying, Come over into Macedonia, and help us . . . ."[2]

The spread of Christianity westward created Western Christendom as we know it today. And you can trace it back to God speaking through a vision.

On another occasion Paul was praying in the temple in Jerusalem, and he "fell into a trance and saw a vision of God saying . . . 'Hurry! Leave Jerusalem, for the people here won't believe you when you give them My message.' "[3] Paul had the audacity to argue with God on that occasion, and again we hear him saying, "But God said to me, 'Leave Jerusalem, for I will send you far away to the *Gentiles!*' "[4]

Paul, Jacob, Joseph, Gideon, Daniel—the list is long and imposing (these are just a few) of those who had dreams and took them seriously. I still don't know what God revealed to me in my dream that made me laugh. God may never reveal it; it may lie buried in my subconscious, never to surface. But I can tell you that the overwhelming grief I had experienced the night before was gone. I went to work that morning knowing what had to be done—God revealed that to me also.

Now just how did He reveal *that* to me? It was at the breakfast table, where I was having a quiet time alone. My husband and son leave at 6:30, so the morning is a wonderful time of day to open the Bible and seek to hear what God is saying to my heart. I always remember what Dr. Bill Bright says in his book *Revolution Now:* "You do not have to prove the Bible; just use it."

I got up from the table a prepared woman. I knew what my instructions from God were for the day. Two hours later I was able to bare my heart to those involved in the problem that had caused such pain the night before. Even though I saw no outward evidence that it had an effect on the hearers, yet in my heart I knew it was the right course of action. I felt right before God and others. The Holy Spirit can be counted upon to prompt us to do that which is right.

We are told to hide God's Word in our hearts[5] and to establish ourselves in the Word.[6] When we do this and act in obedience, we can know what to do in a given situation, and this was my experience that day.

A story is told of Charles Stalker, the noted Quaker evangelist. Alighting from a train, he asked the agent what time the next train came through. The agent replied, "You just got off. Why didn't you stay on?"

Stalker replied, "Some distance from here, I had a deep impression to get off the train which has just gone through and take the next train. I felt that I would have been disobeying the prompting of the Holy Spirit if I had failed to do as I have done."

At that moment, the agent's telegraphic transmitter began to click out a message. The agent turned to Stalker and said, "The train you just got off has been wrecked, with the loss of several lives!"

In speaking of the incident later, Stalker said, "I have long since learned that when God speaks I must obey His voice. The impression came as definitely as though an audible voice spoke to me. Had I disobeyed I might have been among those who were killed."[7]

Bill Bright tells of responding to a strong impression he received which resulted in the founding of

Campus Crusade International. It happened on a spring night in 1951 in his home in the Hollywood Hills:

> The hour was late. A seminary classmate and I were studying together for a Greek examination. Then, God spoke to me in a most illuminating way. It should be explained that God did not speak in audible words, but in a very real way He showed me that I was to devote my full time presenting Christ to collegians. Through developing the campus emphasis, the world could be reached for Christ . . . . That night the plan for reaching the collegiate world for Christ was given to me, and Campus Crusade for Christ International was born.[8]

Dr. Bright explains that it is not easy to share this experience because of the danger of being misunderstood. Furthermore, there are many people who seek experiences to justify what they want to do. We are well-advised not to do this, for the Christian is to live by the principle of faith. Bill Bright, though lacking only a few units for graduation, felt compelled to leave seminary at that time to launch the ministry of Campus Crusade for Christ. Not only did he receive an unusual vision of the work that God was going to entrust to him, but he acted on faith, and the world has since seen what God has done in response to that act of obedience.

In one of Dwight L. Moody's meetings, a man stood and testified, "I am not sure of all the doctrines, and I do not know the Bible very well. There is one thing, however, I am determined to do: I'm going to trust and obey!"

The man's resolution greatly appealed to D.B. Towner, who was conducting the music for Moody's meetings. Later he mentioned it to Rev. J. H. Sammis, a Presbyterian minister.

"Why, that's the heart of Christian living!" Rev. Sammis exclaimed. Before long he wrote the verses of the greatly loved and often-sung hymn "Trust and Obey." Towner composed the music.[9]

One of the first hymns I learned as a child was "Trust and Obey." How much those words have influenced my thinking through the years would be difficult to compute, but I can tell you that the verses and the chorus often come to mind, particularly when I am pressed to make a decision. It has been demonstrated that our "inner child of the past" has a tremendous bearing on our lives as adults. I believe this can have not only some bad effects, but it can produce good results as well. The words to the song go like this:

> *When we walk with the Lord*
> *In the light of His Word,*
> *What a glory He sheds on our way!*
> *While we do His good will*
> *He abides with us still,*
> *And with all who will trust and obey.*

> Chorus:
> *Trust and obey,*
> *For there's no other way*
> *To be happy in Jesus,*
> *But to trust and obey.*

> Last verse:
> *Then in fellowship sweet*
> *We will sit at His feet,*
> *Or we'll walk by His side in the way;*
> *What He says we will do,*
> *Where He sends we will go—*
> *Never fear, only trust and obey.*[10]

Notice that the first verse puts the emphasis on walking with the Lord in the light of His Word, and abiding in that Word. That last verse calls attention to what He says and where He sends—it holds out the promise of hearing Him speak and having His guidance. All this comes about as we *trust and obey.*

Without a doubt, God speaks to us from the Bible. That is *His* Word. I begin with the presupposition that the Word of God is *the* inspired Word: "All Scripture is given by inspiration of God, and is profitable for doctrine, for reproof, for correction, for instruction in righteousness, that the man of God may be complete, thoroughly equipped for every good work."[11] I don't question that.

I was on a radio talk-show where one of the callers made the statement that the Bible is full of contradictions, and therefore how could any intelligent person possibly believe it? The amazing thing is that no other book in all of history has been so viciously attacked as the Bible. People have always tried to discredit it and do away with it. And still it stands the test. Long after its attackers have passed from this world, the Word of God still remains!

I trust it. I seek to be obedient to it. I've been trusting it and obeying it for a long time, and I expect to continue to do that until my dying day.

God produced the Bible through the miracle of inspiration. Two Latin words, *in* and *spiro*, combine to form the word "inspiration." *Spiro* means "to breathe." "Inspiration" can literally be interpreted "in-breathed," and when Timothy tells us it is the "inspiration of God," that means "God-breathed."

Much has been made in Christian magazines and books in recent years about the *verbal plenary inspiration* of the Scriptures. Theologians have no trouble understanding that, but what does it say to the average person who has not had the benefit of theological training? *Plenary* comes from the Latin word *plenus,* meaning "full." "Verbal" comes from the Latin word *verbum,* meaning "word."

The next time you are questioned about the Bible, you can say you believe in the verbal, plenary inspiration of the Scriptures, and that you are affirming that every word (in all 66 books) was written under the direction of the Holy Spirit. Jesus Himself spoke of this verbal inspiration when He said, "Do not think that I have come to destroy the Law or the Prophets. I have not come to destroy but to fulfill."[12]

There are two other words we need to understand if we are to stand in defense of the Word of God. One of those words is "infallible." The dictionary defines "infallible" as "incapable of error; never wrong."

Some people try to distort this to mean that the infallibility of the Word of God pertains only to spiritual and moral truths, but that there are errors in matters pertaining to historical and scientific data, reflecting the culture of the specific writers.

To hold to that view opens the door to all kinds of speculation and misconceptions. Scholars refuting that line of reasoning added another word to describe their belief regarding the inspiration of the Bible. That word is "inerrant," meaning that the Bible is wholly true in everything it teaches; the Word is completely free from error.

All of this is of immense importance as we seek to answer the question, How do we know when God speaks? If we don't understand something in the Word of God, this is not the Bible's fault, but is simply a question of our own limited understanding. We are fallible, liable to be mistaken.

Were the writers of the Bible some kind of super-saints to whom God entrusted messages and told them, "Now these things I'm saying to you are going to be recorded for all posterity in a book that will come to be called the Bible?" These were very normal people, although some of them were men who exhibited what could be called a spectacular kind of faith. I believe that the Holy Spirit moved upon these authors so that they did not make mistakes. If they had the equivalent of erasers to correct mistakes, they didn't need to use them! I believe they wrote as would historians of today, or as songwriters, or as letter-writers. But there was a difference: what they wrote was God-breathed!

Some of the prophets, such as Jeremiah, were told, "Thus speaketh the Lord God of Israel, saying, Write all the words that I have spoken unto thee in a book."[13] Others were given similar messages (2 Chronicles 26:22, Isaiah 8:1; Ezekiel 24:2, 37:16-20; 43:11). Habakkuk was told, "Write the vision . . . ."[14]

In the New Testament, the Book of Hebrews plainly states that in times past God spoke to the prophets in various ways. Then the writer points out that "in these last days" (meaning the times in which he was writing and in days to come) God has spoken through His Son.[15] The prophets received the Word from God in visions, dreams, and even face-to-face, but after Jesus came to earth we no longer see these great prophets striding across the biblical landscape.

Does this mean that God no longer spoke to them (and to succeeding generations) through visions, dreams, prophecies, and encounters of the kind experienced by Moses (Exodus 17:14; 34:1,27; Deuteronomy 31:19)? Not at all. The aim of the writer of Hebrews is to show the superiority of Christ to all other messengers by whom He has revealed His Word. Specifically what is being pointed out is that Christ is the embodiment of God's perfect revelation of Himself.

Whether in the Old Testament or the New Testament, it is still the voice of God; the message is divine. It is good to remember that the New Testament (and Christianity as we have come to understand it) was not designed as a refutation of Judaism; it was to be its completion, its fulfillment.

One other reference should be called to your attention which confirms that the voice of God speaks to us out of the Bible. 2 Peter 1:16-21 says:

> For we have not followed cunningly devised fables when we made known to you the power and coming of our Lord Jesus Christ, but were eyewitnesses of His majesty. For He received from God the Father honor and glory when such a voice came to Him from the Excellent Glory: "This is My beloved Son, in whom I am well pleased."
>
> And we heard this voice which came from heaven when we were with Him on the holy mountain. We also have the prophetic word made more sure, which you do well to heed as a light that shines in a dark place, until the day dawns and the morning star rises in your hearts; knowing this first, that no prophecy of Scripture is of any private interpretation; for prophecy never came by the will of man, but holy men of God spoke as they were moved by the Holy Spirit (NKJB).

People say today, "Oh, if only I could hear God speak audibly! Oh, if only He would talk to us the way He talked to Peter and the other disciples when they were with Him on the mountain!" (See Matthew 17:1-8; Luke 9:35.)

What the Bible is telling us is that Peter and the others heard the best voice that ever came from heaven to earth (telling them that God was pleased with His Son), but that He is also pleased with this One who lives in the believer by the power of the Holy Spirit. God had said, "This is My beloved Son, in whom I am well-pleased. Hear Him!" (Matthew 17:5). But elsewhere the Bible tells us that *we* are accepted in the beloved (Ephesians 1:6).

Because we as Christians accept the fact that the sacred records were divinely inspired and preserved, we can sit at our breakfast tables and hear God speaking to us today. I received instruction as to how to handle the devastating experience mentioned earlier in this chapter. Not to have followed what I was reading in the Bible that morning would have been an act of *not* listening to God speak; it would have been disobedience.

CHAPTER
3

Guidance Through The Writings Of Others

The choice of books, like that of friends, is a serious duty. We are responsible for what we read as what we do.

—John Lubbock

CHAPTER 3

ONE OF MY favorite writers, Sherwood Wirt, had a very interesting interview with C.S. Lewis in 1963 in Cambridge. He asked Lewis the question, "Do you believe that the Holy Spirit can speak to the world through Christian writers today?"

The answer of C.S. Lewis is interesting:

> I prefer to make no judgment concerning a writer's direct "illumination" by the Holy Spirit. I have no way of knowing [whether] what is written is from heaven or not. I do believe that God is the Father of lights— natural lights as well as spiritual lights (James 1:17). That is, God is not interested only in Christian writers as such. He is concerned with all kinds of writing. In the same way a sacred calling is not limited to ecclesiastical functions. The man who is weeding a field of turnips is also serving God.

Dr. Wirt pointed out to Lewis that an American writer had stated that in his opinion the Isaac Watts hymn "When I Survey the Wondrous Cross" was more inspired by God than the Song of Solomon in the Old Testament. To this Lewis replied:

> The great saints and mystics of the church have felt just the opposite about it. They have found tremendous spiritual truth in the Song of Solomon. There is a difference of levels here. The question of the canon is involved. Also we must remember that what is meat for a grown person might be unsuited to the palate of a child.[1]

Lewis' reference to "canon" needs explanation. One of the most helpful explanations of the origin of that word is to be found in *The Criswell Study Bible*. In a section entitled "The Bible: A Book of Destiny," Dr. Paige Patterson writes:

The word "canon" comes from the Greek word (kanōn), meaning literally "reed" and thus "straightedge" or "ruler" or "rod." Out of this association with measurement, the term metaphorically became a reference to a standard. Conservative scholars maintain that every book of the Bible has God as its Author and His authority inherent thereby. The thirty-nine books of the Old Testament are considered canonical by the Jews, the apostolic church, and the Christian churches through the centuries. As applied to Scripture, then, the canon is the list of books which are accepted by the Church as conforming to the standard of divine inspiration and authority and, therefore, as forming a "rule" of faith and practice for every believer.[2]

Working as an editor, I have read letters from people who have written both prose and poetry and submitted them for publication. Sometimes accompanying their manuscript is a letter stating that God told them to write this, that they felt divinely inspired, and that God had told them to tell us (the publisher) that it was not to be changed. We have also had letters informing us that God had revealed to them that we were to be the publisher of that material.

Now this can become downright embarrassing! What can we answer in such a situation? Generally speaking, we have to come right out and say that we didn't get the same message from God (as we return the manuscript with a letter of rejection).

It is not for us to judge whether such people have been moved by the Holy Spirit to write, but it is the prerogative *and* responsibility of publishers to make value judgments on material submitted to them for publication. (Perhaps God intended for them to write it down for their own edification, since writing is a very personally satisfying and edifying experience, but it does not necessarily mean that God intends for it to be published and widely circulated.)

Is God speaking to the world through Christian writers today? This is really not difficult to answer: of course He is. If He hasn't been doing this, then what can we say about those thousands of people who testify that their lives have been dramatically changed as a result of reading a book or a message from a daily devotional, or some other piece of literature? Every writer of Christian literature whom I personally know has related incidents in the lives of people who have communicated with him or her that this has actually happened. It has also been my own experience on more than one occasion.

Many writers feel moved by the Holy Spirit to address themselves to certain issues, and they feel that God's hand has been upon them as they write. Thousands upon thousands of magazines, books, pamphlets—printed messages in whatever form they take—bear a distinctly Christ-centered message and are being used by God to speak to the hearts of readers. There can be no doubt about it—God is still using writers.

However, we must distinguish between original inspiration (the Bible) and the guidance which God holds out to all who ask for it (certainly not limited to those who happen to be skilled in writing). Elisabeth Elliot has addressed herself to this subject of guidance in her book *A Slow and Certain Light.*

> *I have found in the Bible plenty of evidence that God has guided people. I find, too, assurance that He is willing to guide me. He has been at it for a long time. His hand reaches toward me. I have only to take it.*[3]

Those of us who supplement our Bible reading and study with other worthy reading materials have often found ourselves the beneficiaries of the wisdom that God has given to the writers. Who has not read the writings of Corrie ten Boom, including her life story as related in *The Hiding Place*, and not been moved to tears? What parent hasn't been helped immensely as a result of reading James Dobson's *Dare To Discipline*? How many marriages have been helped (some even saved) as a result of the counsel received from the writings of H. Norman Wright, Clyde Narramore, or Tim LaHaye (to mention just a few)? And what are we to say of the God-blessed writings of Catherine Marshall, James Johnson, Dale Evans Rogers, Anita Bryant, Joyce Landorf, Charles Swindoll, Billy Graham, and others? Books are truly among the great ministers that God has given to men. Our lives are immeasurably enriched through the reading of such books.

For as long as I can remember I have been using the daily devotional book *Streams in the Desert*. My first worn and underlined copy was given to my youngest daughter when she called me one day a few years ago to ask for prayer about a personal problem. It was immediately replaced, and I continue to find fresh new help in it every day. I have also made it a practice through the years of giving this book as a gift.

Barbara Johnson has written a book entitled *Where Does A Mother Go To Resign?* Barb lost one son in the Vietnam war, another son was killed in an automobile accident, and son number three chose the homosexual lifestyle. When Barb first made that discovery, she felt like she had been splattered all over the ceiling. She began a ministry which she called "Spatula Ministries" in an effort to help scrape parents and others "off the ceiling."

Barb's book is finding its way into the hands of thousands of people, and the responses of the readers are very revealing. Through her pain and willingness to share the lessons that God has been teaching her, Barb has reached out through writing with the prayerful hope that her book might help others. There is no way of measuring the impact of such honest sharing.

C.S. Lewis gave out plenty of pointers on how to become a better writer, but his most succinct advice for developing good style was to know exactly what you want to say and to be sure you are saying exactly that. Of his own writing he said to the Lord: "If this is rubbish, throw it away. But if it's real, breathe into it." The logic and diversity of his writing express the intensity of his commitment to life, God, and his fellow man. He was a channel through whom God has breathed truth that stands.

A public figure whose journalistic wit made him known internationally is Malcolm Muggeridge. The impact of his life and writings first caught the Christian world's attention with the publication of his book *Jesus Rediscovered*. Sherwood Wirt wrote of him:

> *Malcolm Muggeridge's gift for invective was developed through forty years of journalism in a land where the competition is deadly. His years as a student at Cambridge, as a teacher in India, as a journalist with the Manchester* Guardian, *as a correspondent in Moscow, as editor of* Punch, *as a newspaper correspondent in Washington, D.C., have brought him to ripe maturity with a razor-keen mind that spends much of its time slashing to ribbons the pretensions of his fellowmen.*
>
> *That such a man should be tamed by Jesus Christ is a fresh demonstration of the limitless grace of God. What the Bible did for Muggeridge was to lend his writings coherence, and give his caustic style a frame of reference . . . .*[4]

There are still those who wince when they read some of Muggeridge's writings, but in the years since *Jesus Rediscovered* was published (1971), his words have caught the attention of the world. More than one person can point to Muggeridge's writings and say they have been challenged and helped—yes, even introduced to the Man from Galilee, the "You who are alive," in Muggeridge' own words.

> *I feel as though all my life I've been looking for an alternative scene; for the face behind the cotton wool, the flesh beneath the wax, the light beyond the arc lights, time beyond the ticking of the clocks, a vista beyond the furthermost reach of mortal eyes even when magnified to thousands of light years, for a destiny beyond history. How extraordinary that I should have found it, not in flying up to the sun like Icarus, but in God coming down to me in the Incarnation.*[5]

Many people have been helped and challenged by the example of John Wesley. During the more than 40 years he spent on horseback, he traveled a quarter-million miles! He preached 42,000 sermons and wrote more than 200 books![6]

There must have been many heartaches and disappointments in Wesley's life. On more than one occasion he must have felt that he was "splattered on the roadside": the matrimonial boat of his life rocked back and forth until his wife left him; he came to this country to convert the Indians but left a broken man wallowing in the "slough of despond."

His journal tells his turbulent story. Out of the fiery path that led to self-debasement, Wesley was in a position where God's voice could reach him. He became a spiritual learner, and his strength rested in the fact that he was a man of one Book, and that

Book was the Bible. He wanted only that his life be fully in accord with God, and he called this spiritual alignment "Christian perfection."

This tireless man tutored himself to read while on horseback. As he traveled along the country roads of England on the back of his horse, he would be busy either reading or writing. Often he was stoned; gangs attacked him and dragged him into alleys. He was also frowned upon by the clergy and openly opposed by the bishops.

Out of all this, Wesley developed a following of lay preachers. One of the things he impressed upon them was the necessity of possessing a bookshelved mind. Among the minutes of his meetings with them are the words, "Read the most useful books . . . . Steadily spend all the morning in this employ, or at least five hours in twenty-four." When someone would complain that he had no taste for reading, Wesley would simply say, "Contact a taste for it by use, or return to your trade." John Wesley was trying to make sure there were no preachers who delivered their sermons with a leaden step.[7]

John's brother Samuel tried to dissuade him from his open-air preaching. But John Wesley was listening to the voice of God, as his reply to his brother plainly shows:

> *God in Scripture commands me according to my power to instruct the ignorant, reform the wicked, confirm the virtuous. Man forbids me to do this in another's parish; that is, in effect, to do it at all, seeing I have now no parish of my own, nor probably ever shall. Whom then shall I hear: God or man?*
>
> *I look upon the world as my parish . . . . I shall obey God rather than man.*[8]

For John Wesley, God was the court of last appeals. Wesley's words ring with truth; they should command our attention:

My ground is the Bible. Yes, I am a Bible bigot. I follow it in all things.[9]

A woman who was the director of a large Christian women's organization had her leadership seriously undermined a a result of being open to the movement of the Holy Spirit. Quite new in the faith at the time, this woman felt herself slipping into what she now recalls as an "emotional paralysis."

Early one morning I went alone to my dressing room, and, sinking to my knees, I poured out my heart to God, pleading for help. After a time I rose and stepped through the door into my bedroom. As I did, very distinctly through my mind—my consciousness—went the words, "Why are you worrying? Don't you know that I take care of all these things?"

I needed no one to tell me that it was the voice of God. And with those words it was though someone had opened a window in a totally black room, not all the way, just a tiny bit, but it was enough that a ray of light seemed to penetrate that inner room and my consciousness. With this came a release, a definite lessening of the tension and despair that had enveloped me.

In less than thirty minutes my phone rang. It was a loyal and concerned member of my club board. She had no idea that something was troubling me, as I had confided in no one but my husband. Yet she sensed that something was wrong.

"I have been clearing off the top of my desk," she said, "and I have come across a tract that has been there for some time. I keep having the feeling that God is urging me to read it to you."

"Whatever it is, I need it. Please read it to me," I answered. As she began to read the message from that tract, it was again as though electricity went from my head, through my body, to my feet, and back again. I felt that God was speaking, verifying that this message was from Him. Every word of that message spoke directly to me, meeting my great need, and assuring me that God was aware of the entire problem, and that He would indeed take care of it. There was admonishment, too, as it pointed out that I must let HIM take over, saying that these things were too big for me, and pointing to something in my own attitude that needed correction.

It was a message of comfort and love, and as she finished reading the last words of that message, I knew that I had my answer. God had spoken. I knew, too, the source of my strength and my help in time of need. That little ray of light that had entered my darkness before became a bright shining light, flooding my entire being. I finished my term as president of the club with my head held confidently high, and with God's hand in mine (John 10:27,28). As the years have gone by I have grown in the Word and in spiritual understanding, always aware of His presence and His loving guidance.

How did she hear God's voice? She had been on her knees praying to Him. When Jesus was teaching His disciples how to pray, He said, "But thou, when thou prayest, enter into thy closet, and when thou hast shut thy door, pray to thy Father who is in secret" (Matthew 6:6). Relaxed and still before the Father, she called out to Him. And He heard and answered. Audibly? No, but distinctly in her inner consciousness.

Then, far across town, God nudged one of His choice ones, a co-worker on the same club board, and she heard His voice. Audibly? No, an inner sensitivity had made her aware that someone needed a word, and she responded as God placed in her hands a tract, and without hesitation she made a phone call that transformed another person's life. She became God's mouthpiece.

Can we learn and receive direction from the writings of others?

A word of caution is in order. It is a known fact that it is also possible to be led astray by writings. We should always use *the Word of God* as our measuring rod. Does what the writer say square with Scripture? If there is any doubt in your mind, then proceed with caution if you continue reading the literature.

It would also be wise to seek the counsel and advice of a godly Christian whom you respect. (This could be your pastor or another spiritual mentor.) If you have a good Christian bookstore in your area, you should befriend someone in that store who knows books. You can also learn much about books by following the book review section in reliable Christian magazines.

Church librarians are valuable resource persons, as are Sunday school teachers. There are several Christian TV talk-shows where you can watch authors being interviewed and hear their responses to the questions being asked about them and their writings. Radio talk-shows and Christian broadcasters will frequently call attention to books. In these ways you will learn of many good books. But read with caution, and ask God to give you discernment. Reading can add a new dimension to your spiritual life and growth. Reading Christians are growing Christians. Someone has said that a man is himself plus the food he eats, the friends he makes, and the books he reads.

I spent part of my life working in our Christian bookstores. One day a young mother came into the store with her new baby and asked me to watch the baby while she searched for a certain book. Soon she was back at the counter and handed the book to me. Then she said, "I'm so glad you have this book. Someone gave one to me while I was expecting this little one. God spoke to my heart while reading it, and now my baby has a mother who can tell him about Jesus. I'm buying this as a gift, and I'll be praying that God will use it in her life as He did in mine."

By then tears had formed in my eyes. She had tears as she talked—joyful tears. Then she noticed my expression and my tears. Suddenly it dawned on her. She looked at the book, saw the photo, and exclaimed, "Oh no! You're the author!" We embraced.

This was not only a joyful experience, but it was humbling. It made me very conscious of the need to seek to hear God speaking to me as I wrote. I determined then and there that I would always write what I sensed were need-meeting books. That first book, *Joyfully Expectant: Meditations Before Baby Comes*, had been born out of what I felt was a need: I had given birth to four children, and each time I wanted a book that spoke to me about what God said in regard to childbearing and other truths that would help prepare me for motherhood.

Books can be classified as counselors. To carefully weigh the counsel of others, whether through books or personal counsel, is to draw upon the kind of help we all need in our decision-making. We are ultimately responsible to God for our decisions, but we cannot ignore our responsibility to others. We ourselves can be better prepared to be wise counselors as we fill our minds with that which is true, honest, just, pure, lovely, and of good report—even as the Apostle Paul admonishes in Philippians 4:8.

There is one author who is totally reliable. In the Book of Hebrews we are told to look unto Jesus, "the Author and Finisher of our faith."[10]. The book of all books in the Bible.

CHAPTER

4

Out Of The Mouths Of Babes

I have many times found a clearer knowledge of the gospel and a warmer love toward Christ in the child convert than in the adult convert. I may astonish you by saying that I have sometimes met with a deeper spiritual experience in a child than in some persons fifty or sixty.

—Charles Spurgeon

CHAPTER 4

THOSE WHO have worked with children acknowledge the readiness with which they respond to spiritual truth. F.B. Meyer, famed Bible teacher and author, said, "I am increasingly enamored with children. They have not to unlearn those habits of doubt and misconception which hinder so many from accepting the gospel. It is natural for them to trust One whom they cannot see, to give Him their choicest treasures to conform themselves to His sweet life."

How well I recall a dinnertime conversation with my son Kraig when he was just a little guy. Suddenly he piped up with, "God doesn't speak like us." Momentarily I was caught off-guard.

"What do you mean? What do we speak?"

"We speak English," he answered.

"Okay, so we speak English; how does God speak?"

"God speaks nice."

At the time I considered that a capsule sermon! It ended as abruptly as it had begun, but each word conveyed a meaningful message that set my mind to thinking for several hours afterward. Don't misunderstand; we thought our English-speaking dinnertime conversations were just fine—stimulating and rarely disinteresting. But my five-year-old thought God spoke "nice," and that meant much more than stimulating, interesting, English-speaking family talk.

I had to ask myself just what my child meant. I came to the conclusion that he had recognized God speaking to him in his inner self. Something triggered that remark. What a discovery—to grasp the concept that God communicates with us, and to understand that God is gracious and nice!

I think if I would have asked my small son that day, "Kraig, did you hear God speak?" he would have answered "Yes." If I had prodded further, my child would have said that he did not hear God speak audibly. But he did hear Him speak. Not English as we speak it, but He spoke to my son.

God does speak. He comforts our hearts with the knowledge that comes from His Word. He cheers our spirits—sometimes through others who have heard His voice, and at other times through the message of a song, a book, or a poem. We see His hand at work creatively in a beautiful sunset, a forest of trees, and a rainbow after the rain—and we know that this is God speaking.

Sometimes He speaks loudest when He speaks through the lips of innocence personified in a child. At such times our hearts echo the words of those who heard Him speak in Moses' day, and we too can say, "Today the Lord our God has shown us His glory and greatness; we have even heard His voice. . . ."[1]

As children face the world with their unique optimism, compassion, idealism, and natural sense of humor, their uninhibited remarks speak with depth and discernment to those who truly listen. Many a mother has confessed that she has learned much from her children. No wonder Jesus set a child in the midst of His disciples and said, "Truly, except you turn to God from your sin and become as little children, you will never even get into the Kingdom of Heaven. Therefore anyone who humbles himself as this little child is the greatest in the Kingdom of Heaven."[2]

On still another occasion little children were brought to Jesus. That is not hard to imagine. I think if I had been a mother living in those days, I would have brought my children to Him also. They came asking Jesus to put His hands on their children, and to pray for them. What a tender scene!

The disciples quickly reacted and rebuked the mothers. But Jesus had a word for them. It is a word for us too as we attempt to answer the question: How do you know when God is speaking?

"Permit the little children, and forbid them not to come unto me, for of such is the kingdom of heaven."[3]

In these two incidents, and the statements made, Jesus showed His disciples (and us) the greatness to be found in being willing to take upon one's self the character of a child and all that this implies.

But these are not the only times that Jesus pointed to children to draw attention to something specific He wanted His followers to hear and learn. At the time of His triumphal entry into Jerusalem He went to the temple. There He created a stir which the self-righteous priests and scribes had never seen before. The blind and the lame came to Jesus in the temple, and He healed them. Moreover, the children were running around shouting, "Hosanna to the Son of David!" Just prior to this He had overturned the tables of the moneychangers. What a scene!

The chief priests and scribes were indignant. When they angrily said to Him, "Do You hear what these are saying?" Jesus said to them, "Yes; have you never read, Out of the mouths of children and infants You have made (provided) perfect praise?"[4] His reference was to Psalm 8:2.

What parent wouldn't have to admit that seeing his or her children at prayer and praising God doesn't bring a lump to one's throat and a tear to the eyes! Some of the most precious prayer thoughts ever heard have come from the lips of children. Matthew Henry says that praise is perfected (that is, God is glorified in the highest degree) when strength is ordained out of the mouths of babes.

Sometimes the power of God and His greatness and glory are seen in the most unlikely ways in His church—for example, by the very weak and unlikely instruments of new converts, babes in the things of the Lord.

There comes that moment in each of our lives when we come to what I call "a crossroads experience." Some choose to ignore the inner promptings. But parental religious heritage is no substitute for a personal relationship with God through Christ. In the Bible we find many commands that hold out a promise: "Train up a child in the way he should go, and when he is old, he will not depart from it."[5]

A child may learn this verse: "Behold, I stand at the door and knock; if any man hear my voice and open the door, I will come into him and will sup with him, and he with me."[6] But this verse may not have meaning until the child hears God's voice and responds. He may then open his heart's door and invite Christ in. It is unlikely that the child will have heard an audible voice, yet the verse says, "If any man *hear my voice.*" Child or adult, there must come that time when Christ is given access to the human heart. We must hear Him speak.

I think of the story of Hannah Hurnard, beloved writer of *Hinds' Feet On High Places.* But Hannah was not always a deeply spiritual person, sensitive to the voice of God and His gentle leading. At one time she spoke with "a dreadful stammer." This agonizing handicap led her to also experience tormenting fears—terror of the dark, of heights, of crowds, of being ill, of fainting and losing consciousness, and above all a daily and nightly horror of death. The older she grew, the more she felt the humiliation and hurt of these two things, so that she longed for the courage to commit suicide.

When she was 19 years of age, her father told her he wanted to take her to a convention at Keswick. She was horrified at the thought, but she did go. In her heart she thought, "If there really is a God, surely the Keswick Convention is the place where He is most likely to reveal Himself to me. And if I don't find Him it will be complete confirmation that the whole thing is wishful thinking or delusion."

At the end of that convention, in an extremity of despair and misery of heart, alone in her room she cried out, "Oh God, if there is a God anywhere, You must make Yourself real to me. If You exist and are really what these people describe You to be, You can't leave me like this."

How did God answer that cry? He spoke to her from the Bible. She had been calling to a God who did not answer or respond audibly. In 1 Kings 18 Elijah challenged the Israelites to believe in the one true God, and he declared that he would prove that God existed. This is what spoke to Hannah Hurnard. Life for her was utterly different and radiant from that hour onward. She speaks of it in her writings as being the same Hannah, but in some miraculous and mysterious way she knew she had been lifted into a completely new mental and spiritual environment, out of the dreadful isolation of self-imprisonment and into the love of God.

From the first moment that God made Himself real to her, He led her to the decision that she would speak to Him and ask Him questions, and act in every way as she would if she could actually see Him. She found that she had to keep putting the reality of His presence to the test. And it worked. She spoke to Him with complete naturalness and no artifical phraseology. She made the life-changing discovery that it was obvious God used one's own mental faculties to receive the thoughts He wanted to give. "Sometimes all my faculties were wholly yielded to the Lord and, at that time, I could hear His voice."

An audible voice, Hannah? No, in matters of Christian truth and understanding of God's Word to us, we learn slowly and by stages. Hannah set to work to develop what she called "a hearing heart."

When I read Hannah Hurnard's book *The Hearing Heart* many years ago, I literally jumped with joy. Hannah was voicing what I too had discovered. But hear it from her:

> The great principle of "The Hearing Heart" is that we "become as little children," utterly dependent and always ready to obey. We have to learn to obey His guidance in small personal matters before we can receive and understand more of His will and purposes.

> But we MUST HEAR, or how can God teach us? And learning to hear and to understand and to obey is the most vital thing in Christian experience.[7]

I first encountered the idea that God spoke while hearing my mother sing one of her favorite songs. I learned the words and came to love them too. The words go like this:

I come to the garden alone,
While the dew is still on the roses;
And the voice I hear
Falling on my ear
The Son of God discloses.

Chorus:

And He walks with me
And He talks with me,
And He tells me I am His own;
And the joy we share as we
*   tarry there*
None other has ever known.

He speaks, and the sound of His voice
Is so sweet the birds hush
*   their singing;*
And the melody
That He gave to me
Within my heart is ringing.

I'd stay in the garden with Him
Tho' the night around me be falling,
But He bids me go;
Thru the voice of woe,
His voice to me is calling.[8]

Some years ago Dr. Francis Schaeffer wrote a book entitled *He Is There and He Is Not Silent.* You can be sure I read it with great interest! The book is a challenge to pessimism. God is not a far-off, disinterested God. He is a personal-infinite God. For us to be defensive about the reality of God's being and that He does communicate with us is to take a back seat to the agnostics, the pantheists, and the scoffers (by whatever name they choose to call themselves). No, it is not a time to be defensive; it is a time to communicate clearly to others our own convictions that God is talking—that He is not silent.

If God is silent and we do not seem to be hearing Him speaking, where does the trouble lie? I am reminded of an incident that happened when one of our daughters was little. It was a foggy night. The fog lay heavy in the night air. It was wispy, ghostly stuff. It came rolling in like great ocean waves and made the night appear cottony-wet. Lighted windows looked as if they were wearing damp halos. The air seemed strangely still, and sounds that you would not ordinarily notice sounded distinct and clear. Street lights were the haziest of blurs, and car lights scarcely penetrated the thick white denseness.

As we stepped out of the house, the electric wires were crackling and humming in a most unusual way. Tonia said, "Listen! God's telephone lines are busy!" But they weren't and they aren't.

The lines of communication between an all-hearing heavenly Father and His earthbound children are always open. In the Book of Psalms we read, "O God . . . you have always cared for me in my distress; now hear me as I call again. Have mercy on me. Hear my prayer . . . . Mark this well: The Lord has set apart the redeemed for Himself. Therefore He will listen to me and answer when I call to him."[9]

It is only as we shut off those lines of communication by our own rebellion and wrongdoing that we sever the connection. "I cannot endure iniquity . . . when you spread out your hands in prayer, I will hide my eyes from you; yes, even though you multiply prayers, I will not listen. . . . Remove the evil of your deeds from My sight. Cease to do evil; learn to do good; seek justice. . . ."[10]

No, God doesn't need telephone lines! He is always listening, always watching.

Joan related how a serious accident at her husband's automotive repair shop had resulted in a painful injury to his partner. That evening at the family dinner table everyone bowed his head and heart in prayer for the injured man. After the meal, Kent (almost three) walked to his toy telephone, picked up the receiver, and dialed. He waited a few minutes and said, "Hello, Jesus?" There was a moment of silence, and then, "Will You make Buddy all well? (Pause.) Okay! Thank You, dear Jesus."

Talking to an unseen person on his own, in Kent's limited realm of experience, had included only telephone conversations. It was understandable that in his desire to reach Jesus to intercede on Bud's behalf, little Kent should choose to use the phone. But you know, I'm not so sure he didn't connect with a direct line to heaven! Haven't we been told to call on Him in the day of trouble, and He would deliver us?[11]

In another psalm we are reminded, "He shall call upon me, and I will answer him . . . ."[12]

Job assures us that when we make our prayers to God, he will hear us.[13] Isaiah says that while we are yet speaking, God will hear and answer.[14] The Bible abounds with such references, and it is a rewarding study to pursue and see how God hears and answers. He is not silent.

How it must have delighted the Father-heart of God to receive such a call from a little fellow: "Hello, Jesus?" You can be assured that such childlike faith on your part is what the Lord is looking for today. "Out of the mouth of babes. . . ."

Arthur T. Pierson, in his biography *George Müeller of Bristol*, relates that God gave Müeller a very simple, childlike disposition toward Himself:

> *In many things he was in knowledge and in strength to outgrow childhood and become a man, for it marks immaturity when we err through ignorance and are overcome through weakness. But in faith and in the filial spirit, he always continued to be a little child. Mr. J. Judson Taylor well reminds us that while in* nature *the normal order of growth is from childhood to manhood and so to maturity, in* grace *the true development is perpetually backward toward the cradle: we must become and continue as little children, not losing, but rather gaining, childlikeness of spirit. The disciple's maturest manhood is only the perfection of his childhood. George Müeller was never so really, truly, fully a little child in all his relations to his Father as when in the ninety-third year of his age.*[15]

CHAPTER
5

An Understanding Mind And A Hearing Heart

We must always be absolutely honest both with God and with ourselves. Never, never must we get into the habit of rationalizing or persuading ourselves that something is right or permissible when God tells us that it is not. Never must we allow wishful thinking to take the place of God's will and voice. —Hannah Hurnard [1]

CHAPTER 5

DR. JAMES I. Packer, much respected theologian and noted author, in discussing knowing God and gaining a grip on His wisdom and ours, uses the illustration of learning to drive. What matters in driving is the speed and appropriateness of your reaction to things, and the soundness of your judgment in various situations. You simply try to do the right thing in each situation that presents itself. The effect of divine wisdom is to enable you and me to do just that in the actual situations of everyday life. To drive well, we must keep our eyes open to notice exactly what is in front of us. To live wisely, we must be clear-sighted and realistic—ruthlessly so—in looking at life as it is.[2]

We have a responsibility before God and others to make careful decisions. John Donne was right: no man is an island. Most of our decision-making touches the lives of others. In seeking to respond to God's voice, we need to heed the guidance that is specifically spelled out for us in the Bible. Solomon called this *wisdom*.

Dr. George Sweeting of Moody Bible Institute says that God is not some celestial Dictator who wants to order every movement of our lives. It really makes little difference to Him if we drive a Chevrolet, Ford, Plymouth—or no car at all. He does not wish to tell us what color tie to wear. He is very deeply interested in us, and in all that we do, but He also wants us to use our own sanctified, God-given common sense.[3]

Almost everyone with whom I corresponded and asked how God speaks referred to the thought process that goes on within the mind. Dr. Bill Bright speaks of this as sanctified reasoning, and a balanced, disciplined mind. It helps to remember this as we seek to know whether it is God who is speaking. None of us wants to be guilty of letting our subconscious mind project itself as the guidance of God.

M. Blaine Smith, a minister serving as director of an organization called Nehemiah Ministries, Inc., has written an illuminating book entitled *Knowing God's Will*, with the subhead "Biblical Principles of Guidance." He stresses that God takes the initiative in guidance, and that our main responsibility is to be in close communion with Him; and that prayer, more than anything, is the channel through which we develop and maintain an openness to the will of God. But we are also to use our heads. I call this developing an understanding mind and a hearing heart.

I first grasped this while reading the Psalms. There I came across that verse which is so familiar: "I will instruct you and teach you in the way which you should go; I will counsel you with My eye upon you. Do not be as the horse or as the mule, which have no understanding, whose trappings include bit and bridle to hold them in check."[4]

We do have a responsibility to use our reasoning capabilities to help make logical choices in conformity with God's will. This should not be confused with purely intuitive impressions of His guidance. Here is where we often find ourselves the most perplexed. Smith points out that complex decisions cannot be fully resolved simply through biblical principles.

Matters pertaining to moral decisions are clearly spelled out in the Bible; this should not present a problem for the committed Christian. These are principles which are not difficult to understand. But there are other decisions we are constantly being required to make which the Bible doesn't spell out precisely. These are the times when we are tempted to say, "Oh, if only God would speak audibly; if only I could actually hear His voice!"

Smith underscores that the Bible plays a role in complex decision-making as it influences our thinking to develop the capacity to know God's mind, to grasp His very heart. Knowing the Scriptures acquaints us with the ways and thoughts of

God, so that the Holy Spirit has maximum freedom to guide us in God's will.

> *How blessed is the man who does not walk in the counsel of the wicked, nor stand in the path of sinners, nor sit in the seat of scoffers! But his delight is in the law of the Lord, and in His law he meditates day and night. And he will be like a tree firmly planted by streams of water, which yields its fruit in its season, and its leaf does not wither; and in whatever he does, he prospers (Psalm 1:1-3 NASB).*

(This is not referring to prosperity by the world's standards. It is a reference to fruitfulness for Christ as one lives his life in line with God's will.)

The five logical ways in which Scripture helps us in complex decision-making are these:

1. *Studying Scripture deepens our consciousness of God, thereby helping us to concentrate on Him.*

2. *Studying Scripture brings us into contact with God (when we read with a prayerful spirit). We are doing more than reading facts—we are allowing ourselves to hear God speak.*

3. *The Scriptures inform us of God's principles (biblical norms).*

4. *Biblical passages may confirm a particular decision. We may experience a sense of inspiration to do what the passage is talking about (taking a passage in context and being moved by the Spirit to do what it says). This inspiration should always be checked against other considerations of guidance.*

5. *Finally, the Bible can be an invaluable aid in praying for guidance. In the Psalms we find*

> quite a few prayers for guidance which can
> be read as our own prayer when seeking
> God's will.[5]

If you have never done what the number 5 suggestion says, you have missed a real blessing.

Our need is for discernment, for wisdom. Whenever I think of discernment, I think of Solomon's conversation with God (in a dream). God said to him, "Ask what I shall give thee."[6]

Solomon answered by speaking of David, his father, remembering how he walked before God in truth, in righteousness, and in uprightness of heart. Solomon felt as though he were but a little child in comparison to his father's greatness. He sensed not only that he lacked experience, but, even more important, that he lacked wisdom. As Solomon thought about the multitude of people over whom he was to rule, he acknowledged his own deficiency. Remember, Solomon was thinking these thoughts in his sleep. Notice his intelligent choice. (He could have asked God for anything!)

"Give therefore thy servant an understanding heart to judge thy people, that I may discern between good and bad."[7] The Amplified Bible translates this, "So give Your servant an understanding mind and a hearing heart."

You really can't beat that for asking wisely! We are told that Solomon's request pleased the Lord, and he was given not only a wise and an understanding heart, but also riches and honor. Moreover, he was given the promise of a long life.[8]

The record of Solomon's life is that of a man unequalled in judging and ruling wisely. He possessed both insight and foresight. Would you like to know how he attained such wisdom? Let's listen to Solomon as he reveals how to go about receiving such wisdom:

> *How does a man become wise? The first step is to trust and reverence the Lord! Only fools refuse to be taught.*[9]

Solomon is recalling the words of his father, David, who told him, "Learn to be wise . . . and develop good judgment and common sense! I cannot over-emphasize this point." And Solomon goes on to say:

> *Determination to be wise is the first step toward becoming wise! And with your wisdom, develop common sense and good judgment. If you exalt wisdom, she will exalt you.*[10]
> *For the reverence and fear of God are basic to all wisdom. Knowing God results in every other kind of understanding.*[11]

How can we get to know God that way? Through listening ears and hearing hearts! The best way to come into that kind of understanding is to have our life ruled by what we hear God saying to us, and the most reliable source for gathering such information is from the Bible. We need to be ruled by what we read.

The Apostle Paul told the Colossian Christians, "Let the word of Christ dwell in you richly in all wisdom."[12] And to young Timothy, his son in faith, he wrote, "Continue in the things which you have learned and been assured of, knowing from whom you have learned them, and that from childhood you have known the Holy Scriptures, which are able to make you wise."[13]

You can't improve on that! "Soak yourself in the Bible," Paul is saying. The people to whom he was writing had only the Old Testament. Think how privileged we are to have both the Old and New Testaments! We find ourselves in a quandry, baffled in our decision-making, and we yearn for easy answers—an audible voice would do beautifully, we think. We struggle to sort out our feelings. "Do I give up my present job and uproot my family and move 2,000 miles away?" "Should I enroll in the state university, or go to an out-of-state college, which will end up costing me more?" A homemaker faced with the spiraling costs of living turns to her husband and says, "I can go back to work. Should I?" The head of the house looks at his shrinking paycheck and ponders, "How are we going to make ends meet?"

How much we need wisdom and discernment! We live in a time when complex situations confront us on every side. No wonder the Holy Spirit, as the finger of God, wrote through men like Solomon, Paul, and others, cautioning, "See then that you walk circumspectly, not as fools but as wise, redeeming the time, because the days are evil. Therefore do not be unwise, but understanding what the will of the Lord is."[14]

Wisdom recognizes that we walk by faith, not sight. One of God's ways of keeping us humble and in touch with Him is to teach us this walk of faith which requires that we be sensitive to what He is saying. We have a right, as His children, to remind Him of His promises to guide us. We qualify for His instruction and guidance as we trust in Him and place ourselves under His care by a right relationship to Him. Obedience follows.

It helps to think of God as an understanding heavenly Father. This means that we can voice our needs to Him in much the same way as a child comes to his earthly father with requests. The child confidently expects his father to answer. Just so, our attitude should be one of trusting receptivity.

Having this God-consciousness relieves us of overanxiety about whether God will or will not give direction as we face decisions. Hasn't He promised to guide us? Can't He be taken at His

Word? Then why be anxious! Doesn't God want us to be satisfied? Fulfilled? Joyful and happy? A.W. Tozer once made the observation that in almost everything that touches our everyday life on earth, God is pleased when we are pleased. "As a father pitieth his children, so the Lord pitieth them that fear him. For he knoweth our frame."[15]

Can we learn that God takes the responsibility for helping us to hear Him speak? One of the illustrations that Jesus gave His disciples was that of a shepherd. In John 10, Jesus portrays himself as the Good Shepherd. "And when he brings out his own sheep, he goes before them; and the sheep follow him, for they know his voice" (v. 4 NKJB)

It is characteristic of sheep not to know where they are going. Sheep need a shepherd. So it is with us. God, who made us, knows the confusion that sometimes exists in our minds as we seek to hear His voice. What does a good shepherd do? He gently leads his sheep; he takes them to green pastures; yes, he leads them beside still waters. Even so, our great Good Shepherd takes the initiative to make sure that we hear Him when He speaks. His concern for us is even greater than our desire to hear Him.

God has perfect knowledge of us, His sheep. The purpose of the Good Shepherd toward His sheep is one of unselfish and devoted love and discipline. So long as we have a heart that is determined to understand God's will, and ears that are listening to hear His voice, then our fears about not hearing are unjustified.

Sometimes sheep stray from the path and from the green pastures. We are like that. And God does give us liberty and a free will; we can be like wayward sheep. Sin can cause us to deviate from God's perfect will. What then? Jesus gave His disciples an illustration of the shepherd's role which answers that question.

> *What do you think? If a man has a hundred sheep, and one of them goes astray, does he not leave the ninety-nine and go to the mountains to seek the one that is straying?*
>
> *And if he should find it, assuredly, I say to you, he rejoices more over that sheep than over the ninety-nine that did not go astray. Even so . . . your Father (Mathew 18:12-14 NKJB).*

Furthermore, God has shown us through the examples of biblical personalities that even when they veered from following His perfect will, and did not hear Him speak, they were not beyond His reach or hopelessly beyond hearing Him calling to them.

God is pledged to guide us. We should take heart from that. I'm thankful that God doesn't give up on us when we don't hear His voice, or hear but don't obey. The biblical record shows us God's forgiveness when we are contrite and willing to hear Him speak. God's redemptive mercy is beyond the grasp of our comprehension; we know we do not deserve it.

If we are going to be God-guided persons, we must be willing to be guided not to *our* ends but to *God's* purposes.

Elihu, one of Job's friends, said in a lengthy dissertation, "For God speaks again and again. In dreams, in visions of the night when deep sleep falls on men as they live on their beds. He opens their ears in times like that, and gives them wisdom and instruction."[16]

I need that kind of wisdom; you need that kind of wisdom. It isn't going to make us all-wise (only God is that), but it will work to perfect our relationship with Him. It will also show in our relationships with others. James 3:13, 17, 18 has something to say about that:

> *Who is wise and understanding among you? Let him show by good conduct that his works are done in the meekness of wisdom. . . . The wisdom that is from above is first pure, then peaceable, gentle, willing to yield, without partiality, and without hypocrisy. And the fruit of righteousness is sown in peace by those who make peace (NKJB).*

I often remind myself that God is not the Author of confusion (1 Corinthians 14:33). If God is not the Author of confusion, then what can we expect in its place? Peace.

> *Be anxious for nothing, but in everything by prayer and supplication with thanksgiving let your requests be made known to God; and the peace of God, which surpasses all understanding, will guard your hearts and minds through Christ Jesus.*[17]

When weighing alternatives in coming to a decision, in the final analysis I have had to recognize that so long as there is uncertainty and a great deal of perplexity, this is God warning me, or else I would experience peace. Some people may regard this as a very simplistic view, but I know there are times when God disturbs our thinking to give us conviction. I've had this happen often enough to recognize that this is one way God speaks to me. The peace that God gives can be depended upon to keep our thoughts and our hearts quiet. The Amplified Bible refers to it as "a tranquil state . . . fearing nothing . . . and content with its earthly lot . . . which transcends all understanding . . . and garrisons and mounts guard" over our hearts and minds.

Ben Kinchlow relates how he hears God speaking:

> *Whenever you get at cross-purposes with God's direction, or God's plan for your life, you'll find*

*this frustration beginning to build, because
man is made for obedience; he is made to align
himself with God's purpose.*

*I never heard God speaking in an audible
voice, but I certainly have heard Him speaking
to me in the Spirit, His voice translates itself into thought concepts that I can conceive in my
mind. So when I say, "I heard the Lord" or
"the Lord spoke to me," I mean He spoke to me
through a feeling in my spirit that was
translated into a thought in my mind.*

Any lessening of one's peace and tranquility in
God should lead one to question whether God was
the source of the leading.

Dr. Bill Bright, in seeking to give counsel to
students and adults about how to know the will of
God for one's life, refers to what he calls the
"sound-mind principle" of Scripture. He is referring to 2 Timothy 1:7, where we are told that "God
has not given us the spirit of fear, but of power and
of love and of a sound mind." He explains this as
meaning a well-balanced mind—a mind that is
under the control of the Holy Spirit, "remade" according to Romans 12:1, 2:

*Therefore, my brothers, I implore you by
God's mercies to offer your very selves to Him:
a living sacrifice, dedicated and fit for His ac-
ceptance, the worship offered by mind and
heart. Adapt yourselves no longer to the pattern of the present world, but let your minds be
remade and your whole nature thus transformed. Then you will be able to discern the
will of God, and to know what is good, acceptable, and perfect (New English Bible).*

We are well-advised not to base our decisions on
unpredictable emotions and chance circumstances.
Neither should we expect some dramatic or cata-

clysmic revelations from God by which He will reveal His will to us. Dr. Bright says that we do not need to minimize the importance of feelings, but that more emphasis needs to be placed upon this important principle of the sound mind. He points to multitudes of Christians who are wasting their lives, immobile and impotent, as they wait for some unusual or dramatic message from God. "A Christian who has yielded his life fully to Christ can be assured of sanctified reasoning, and a balanced, disciplined mind."

We should be teaching our children to think with their minds. By that I mean *don't be afraid to think, and don't be unwilling to think; be willing to think ahead.* Weigh the long-term consequences of your decisions. Several verses of Scripture support this:

> *Delight thyself also in the Lord, and he shall give thee the desires of thy heart. Commit thy way unto the Lord; trust also in him, and he shall bring it to pass.*[18]

> *Trust in the Lord with all thy heart, and lean not unto thine own understanding. In all thy ways acknowledge him, and he shall direct thy paths.*[19]

> *O that they were wise . . . that they would consider their latter end!*[20]

A good question to ask is why a particular course of action, or a certain choice, seems right. Then we need to be able to answer that question with good reasons that are not contradictory to the Bible. We have a biblical precedent for this in Psalm 139:23,24:

> *Search me, O God, and know my heart; try me, and know my thoughts, and see if there be any wicked way in me, and lead me in the way everlasting.*

An old Scandinavian translation of that word "search" reads "ransack" (my thoughts).

At such times of indecision the counsel of faithful friends whose judgment we trust can be of great help. Sometimes we are so close to the forest that we cannot see the trees. We need someone who can look at our situation from a more objective stance.

> Listen to advice and accept instruction, that you may gain wisdom for the future.[21]

The practical advice of Proverbs is indispensable as we seek to hear God speak.

> Many are the plans in a man's heart, but the counsel of the Lord will stand.[22]

> The spirit of man is the lamp of the Lord, searching all the innermost parts of his being.[23]

We come back to where this chapter began. Our thought processes, our sanctified reasoning, and a balanced, disciplined mind are all involved as we come to God to hear Him speak to us. This is the Infinite speaking to the finite. This is the unlimited, all-powerful God speaking to us—limited men and women. But the hearing ear and the listening heart were both made by God. And we can hear Him speak. He is not the Author of confusion, and He does give peace.

> Thou wilt keep him in perfect peace, whose mind is stayed on thee, because he trusteth in thee.[24]

CHAPTER

6

The Holy Spirit As
A Sure Guide

*The pressure of the inward Spirit of
God upon your life will direct you into His will! The inward witness of
the Spirit—and what a precious gift
it is—is sure to be there in the sur-
rendered life.*

—Alan Redpath[1]

CHAPTER 6

GOD HAS revealed to me that you don't have the Holy Spirit in your life."

Merely to write those words today brings sadness—sadness not for myself, but for those who would make that statement to another person. The sting of the initial hurt is gone, and the memory doesn't linger, but I must recall it now if I am to convey to you why I seriously question that some people who say "God revealed to me" or "God said" are necessarily in communication with God.

That day, some years ago, I was cut to the quick. There are many in the body of Christ who are what I call "the walking wounded." In one way or another they have been deeply hurt by someone—either a well-meaning fellow Christian, or someone whom we might rightly question is a part of the body, or someone who has stepped outside the will of God. It is the latter two groups whom a lot of us have discovered are saying, "God told me. . . ."

The Bible cautions that in the latter days false teachers will abound. Satan is a master counterfeiter. The Bible warns that Satan and his helpers will assail us disguised as "angels of light" (2 Corinthians 11:14). The Apostle Paul calls them "false prophets, deceitful workers, transforming themselves into apostles of Christ."

Counterfeit prophets existed in Old Testament times; they wore the garb and learned the language of the true prophets. Such counterfeits existed in New Testament times as well. We should not be surprised at this. The result of these false teachers will always be ultimate havoc among those who have been lured by their corrupt teachings. It is a pitiful thing to see people ensnared by the counterfeits. Their pretentious claims can only lead to their eventual doom in accordance with their deeds.

· In recent years the world has seen what a Jim Jones can accomplish. Beware of those who come at you claiming superior spiritual knowledge with their "God-revealed-to-me" pronouncements. I cringe inwardly when someone expresses himself as having had an audience with the Eternal, leaving the impression that he has inside information not available to you. In speaking to the Corinthian Christians, Paul at one point said, "Are you beginning to imagine that the Word of God originated in your Church, or that you have a monopoly of God's truth?"[2]

Once again we are brought face-to-face with the need to be wise in the Word so that we can judge what is being said. Do not surrender your knowledge of what God has said to you to someone whose leading puts questions in your mind. Consult with others whose lives show that they know the truth of God. But supremely, let your reliance be on the Word of God.

That day, as I retreated to the Word of God, the Holy Spirit spoke comfort to my wounded spirit. It was at that time that the need for this book presented itself to my heart. I wondered how many others had suffered under the sting of such words. Such insensitivity has reared its ugly head many times; many people have forfeited their relationship with God (though it may have been a weak relationship to begin with, or they may not have been so easily ensnared by the self-righteous pronouncements of another person).

In Chapter 2 I referred to 2 Peter 1, where Peter talks about the trustworthy prophetic word and underscores that "no prophecy of Scripture is of any private interpretation" (v. 20). The interpretation put upon certain portions of the Bible by those who claim superior spiritual gifts and knowledge has brought division to the church.

We are safe when we stay with the Bible and what it says. Those who insist on interpreting certain passages to mean what was never intended, and attempt to snare others into believing it their way, will have to answer to the great Judge of the universe someday. To tamper with the Holy Spirit is to tread on sacred ground. Such people will often refer to the Holy Spirit as "It." "Do you have 'It?' " By this they are referring to a particular gift of the Spirit. To them this gift is the ultimate manifestation of being filled with the Holy Spirit.

What does the Bible have to say about this? I shall let the Word of God stand for itself.

As recorded in John 16:13-15 TLB, Jesus introduced the disciples to the Holy Spirit by saying:

> When the Holy Spirit, who is truth, comes, he shall guide you into all truth, for he will not be presenting his own ideas, but will be passing on to you what he has heard. He will tell you about the future. He shall praise me and bring me great honor by showing you my glory. All the Father's glory is mine; this is what I mean when I say that he will show you my glory.

Jesus never referred to the Holy Spirit as "It." The Holy Spirit is the third *Person* of the Trinity.

Those who anxiously seek for the power of the Holy Spirit are unduly concerned about having "the gifts." When they claim to have received "the gift," we can look at their lives to determine if they are manifesting the *fruit* of the Spirit. It is a very simple test, outlined by the Apostle Paul:

> But when the Holy Spirit controls our lives he will produce this kind of fruit in us: love, joy, peace, patience, kindness, goodness, faithfulness, gentleness and self-control. . . . If we are living now by the Holy Spirit's power, let us follow the Holy Spirit's leading in every part of our lives.[3]

Just prior to speaking these words, the apostle points out the opposite effects in the life of those who follow their own inclinations rather than being guided by the Holy Spirit. The list includes "the feeling that everyone else is wrong except those in your own little group—and there will be wrong doctrine. . . ."⁴

In the Book of Ephesians, Paul begs his readers to "Try always to be led along together by the Holy Spirit, and so be at peace with one another. We are all parts of one body; we have the same Spirit. . . ."⁵ His plea is for *unity in the body.* This plea needs to be sounded loud and clear.

Paul's words to the Galatian Christians assured them that "all of us as Christians can have the promised Holy Spirit through this faith."⁶ "And because we are his sons, God has sent the Spirit of his Son into our hearts, so now we can rightly speak of God as our dear Father."⁷

Jene Wilson of Wilson Family Living, Inc. (Santa Ana, California) makes the point that if someone is doing something that is lifting up the Holy Spirit and calling attention continually to the Holy Spirit, at that point he or she is violating what the Scriptures say the Holy Spirit is actually supposed to do. The Holy Spirit's ministry is to *lift up Jesus Christ.* If we are trying to put the focus on the Holy Spirit Himself, it's no wonder that people are repelled. *They are not being drawn to Jesus,* but are being alienated by an improper approach to what it really means to be a Christian.

What is the purpose of the Holy Spirit? Jesus said it: He is to mold us to become like Jesus.

The teachings regarding the gifts and receiving certain special abilities are not difficult to understand. God has assigned such gifts to each of us, but we don't all have the same gifts. (See Hebrews 2:4; 1 Corinthians 2:10-16; chapters 12,13,14.)

As I sought to understand the Bible and its teachings on the Holy Spirit, I turned to 1 Peter 1:2:

God the Father chose you long ago and knew you would become his children. And the Holy Spirit has been at work in your hearts, cleansing you with the blood of Jesus Christ and making you to please him. May God bless you richly and grant you increasing freedom from all anxiety and fear (TLB).

How do you know when God is speaking? There is no more reliable source for making this determination than in His written Word to you.

First John 2 speaks of "against-Christ people who used to be members of our churches" but who left (see verse 19.) First John 2:20,21,24,27 TLB says:

But you are not like that, for the Holy Spirit has come upon you, and you know the truth. So I am not writing to you as to those who need to know the truth, but I warn you as those who can discern the difference between true and false. So keep on believing what you have been taught from the beginning. If you do, you will always be in close fellowship with both God the Father and his Son. But you have received the Holy Spirit and he lives within you, in your hearts, so that you don't need anyone to teach you what is right. For he teaches you all things, and he is the Truth, and no liar; and so, just as he has said, you must live in Christ, never to depart from him.

My search led me still further into what Peter was saying: First Peter 3:15-18 TLB says:

Quietly trust yourself to Christ your Lord, and if anybody asks why you believe as you do, be ready to tell him, and do it in a gentle and respectful way. Do what is right; then if men speak against you . . . they will become ashamed of themselves for falsely accusing you when you have only done what is good. Remember, if God wants you to suffer, it is better to suffer for doing good than for doing wrong!

I came across these words of Peter that I have since used over and over again. What a rewarding search this proved to be!

. . . . trust yourself to the God who made you, for he will never fail you (1 Peter 4:19b TLB).

This is God speaking, providing all that we need for reassurance, comfort, and help.

. . . if our consciences are clear, we can come to the Lord with perfect assurance and trust, and get whatever we ask for because we are obeying him and doing the things that please him. And this is what God says we must do: Believe on the name of his Son Jesus Christ, and love one another. Those who do what God says—they are living with God and he with them. We know this is true because the Holy Spirit he has given us tells us so (1 John 3:21-24 TLB).

Dearly beloved friends, don't always believe everything you hear just because someone says it is a message from God: test it first to see if it really is. For there are many false teachers around, and the way to find out if their message is from the Holy Spirit is to ask: Does it really agree that Jesus Christ, God's Son, actually became man with a human body? If so, then the message is from God. If not, the message is not from God but from one who is against Christ, like the "Antichrist" you have heard about who is going to come, and his attitude of enmity against Christ is already abroad in the world (1 John 4:1-3 TLB).

. . . you belong to God and have already won your fight with those who are against Christ,

because there is someone in your hearts who is stronger than any evil teacher in this wicked world. These men belong to this world, so, quite naturally, they are concerned about worldly affairs and the world pays attention to them. But we are children of God; that is why only those who have walked and talked with God will listen to us. Others won't. That is another way to know whether a message is really from God; for if it is, the world won't listen to it (1 John 4:4-6 TLB).

. . . . since God loved us . . . we surely ought to love each other too. For though we have never yet seen God, when we love each other God lives in us and his love within us grows ever stronger. And he has put his own Holy Spirit into our hearts as proof to us that we are living with him and he with us . . . (1 John 4:11-13 TLB).

So we have these three witnesses: the voice of the Holy Spirit in our hearts, the voice from heaven at Christ's baptism, and the voice before he died. And they all say the same thing: that Jesus Christ is the Son of God (1 John 5:8 TLB).

The best commentary on the Word of God is the Word itself. One could muster the voices of some of the great writers and theologians to support one's convictions in a situation such as I encountered (where someone claimed that God revealed to him that I did not have the Holy Spirit), but in the final analysis the authority that surpasses all others is what the Bible reveals. This is what I have felt compelled to share in this chapter.

When you are unjustly accused, remember to flee to the Word for the strength necessary to keep your balance. It works every time. An unknown

poet penned these lines which are meaningful in
situations like this:

> Men may misjudge thy aim,
> Think they have cause to blame,
> Say "thou are wrong."
> Keep on thy quiet way:
> Christ is the Judge, not they;
> Fear not, be strong.

CHAPTER
7

Feeling The Power
Of The Voice From Heaven

*Child of my love, fear not the
unknown morrow, Dread not the
new demand life makes of thee; Thy
ignorance doth hold no cause for
sorrow; Since what thou knowest
not is known to me.*
                    —*Author unknown*

CHAPTER 7

IT MAY SEEM that what I am about to tell you now may contradict much of what I have said up to this point. But please do not judge until you have read the entire chapter.

"Go home and look in your mailbox."

I was working in the Salinas, California, library. The hours were long and the job unchallenging. I welcomed the noon break as an opportunity to refresh my thinking with inspirational reading while eating my lunch. This particular day as I made my way to get my book and lunch, I had the strong impression that I should go home and look in the mailbox.

"How ridiculous," I said to myself. Then I "heard" it again. *"Go home and look in your mailbox."*

Decidedly irritated with myself for even entertaining such a suggestion, I nevertheless proceeded to my car. All the way home I argued with myself. I pulled up to the mailbox and opened it. Inside was one letter. I looked at the return address and then hurriedly ripped it open. To my astonishment, inside was a check. I looked at it and gasped.

I ran inside the house, dialed my husband at school, and excitedly told him, "You won't believe it, you just won't believe it!"

Several weeks before this we had received notice that our property taxes were due. (We had assumed that they were included in our monthly payment.) To be suddenly hit with yearly property taxes came as a blow. I had gone back to work to help out with our financial dilemma. Now suddenly I held in my hands the exact amount we needed. It was unbelievable, yet it was true.

We had no reason to even hope for any extra money coming our way. Book royalties had already been paid and had helped pay our living expenses. I read the letter enclosed with the check and learned that one of my publishers had made a mistake in my royalty accounting the previous year, and the mistake had just now been discovered.

From the moment we had learned of the property-tax dilemma until the moment I looked in the mailbox, we had been asking God to provide some answer to our need. The deadline for paying the taxes was upon us, and we seemed no closer to a solution than the day we learned of the problem.

I was able to take the check to the bank that noon, deposit it, and make the tax payment. If I had not heeded the inner prompting and listened to that "still, small voice" (which at the time seemed rather persistent), we would have missed the joy of knowing what it means to hear God speak. Moreover, we would have been a day late in meeting our financial obligation.

Did I hear an audible voice? No, it was not something my ear heard, but my inner mind got the message. I was like the reluctant Jonah, not wanting to go to Ninevah. Jonah finally heeded the word that the Lord was giving to him, and so did I. My failure to sense that God was trying to get through to me provided a lesson which was to make me more sensitive in the days ahead to these nudges of the Holy Spirit.

God will open our ears of understanding to receive what we need to hear if we will live expectantly. So often we pray and seek His direction and help, but we fail to believe not only that He has heard, but that He will help.

There is a very interesting account in Acts 22 of Paul retelling his experience on the Damascus road. His audience was made up of people who understood Hebrew (Acts 21:40). These were fellow Jews (from Asia) who instigated Paul's arrest in the temple at Jerusalem. They were an unruly mob. As Paul tells of the blinding light from heaven, and how he fell to the ground when he encountered Jesus, we hear Paul say, "And those who were with me indeed saw the light, and were afraid, but they did not hear the voice of Him who spoke to me."[1]

Matthew Henry observes:

> *Blessed are those who not only hear but understand; who believe the truth and feel the power of the voice from heaven.*[2]

"So then faith comes by hearing, and hearing by the word of God,"[3] Paul wrote to the Christians at Rome. He was speaking of the necessity for the gospel to be preached to both Jews and Gentiles. But I would imagine that Paul was remembering the dramatic way in which he first heard.

To the church at Thessalonica Paul wrote:

> *For this reason we also thank God without ceasing, because when you received the word of God which you heard from us, you welcomed it not as the word of men, but as it is in truth, the word of God, which also effectively works in you who believe.*[4]

This "word" is like a beautiful skein of gold thread in a fabric, with the gold standing out impressively.

As Paul was speaking to the angry mob of people, he related how he had seen the brilliant light and heard the voice of God, and then had cried out, "What shall I do, Lord?" Imagine this determined man, who was on his way to persecute the Christians, now being stopped in his tracks. God certainly had to resort to a dramatic method of gaining Paul's attention!

What Paul was saying to the Lord, in effect, was, "Let the same voice from heaven that has stopped me in the wrong way now guide me into the right way." It was a plea for help that God answered, as biblical history shows. Paul had felt the power of the voice from heaven.

God has His ways of getting our attention. Sometimes I am very slow to get the message, but God is persistent and patient.

Several people have shared with me that they have felt this persistence on the part of God to get their attention. One woman described it as "a thought being dropped into my mind. I wait . . . and it persists—a thought with an almost nagging quality about it, something I should do or should not do. Perhaps it relates to something I should study or read. If I feel wary as to where this thought is coming from, Matthew 18:16 says, 'In the mouth of two or three witnesses let every word be established.' So corroboration starts cropping up all over—in books, in conversations with other believers, and repeatedly in Scripture. I have found one thing to be absolutely sure—the nudgings of the Holy Spirit are always in line with Scripture. God does not contradict Himself. Sometimes I actively search to see if these things fall in order. Sometimes I wait. But if I really seek to obey Him, He will return again and again, never impatient, but sometimes insistent, for I can be a laggard. But always His proddings are with love."

Hazel King finished her thoughts on this by stating, "I am amazed and humbled that the God who formed us from the dust, who engineered the world, who, as Isaiah prophesied '. . . sits above the vault of the earth, and its inhabitants are like grasshoppers . . .' (Isaiah 40:22 NASB), desires to commune with us. With you. With me. And He does."

Dr. E. Stanley Jones emphasizes that when our ears are trained, we can learn to understand the voice of God within. We will experience a grand liberty from enslaving emotions that are out of character with the nature and purpose of God as revealed in Christ.

It is possible to ignore that inner voice, to our own peril or to the plight and even the peril of others. Marvin Horton experienced this. He speaks of it in the opening chapter of his wife's book, *Dear Mamma, Please Don't Die.*

> *On the day I found my wife nearly dead from an overdose of sleeping pills, I had strong impressions to go home from church early. The impression was illusive at first—Marvin, go home—but it caused me concern. Let me say right here that I'm not given to hearing voices, nor am I very sensitive to inner suggestions; but this whole Easter Sunday morning was strange—contrary to my cool, orderly way of thinking and acting.*
>
> *It wasn't strange that I was in church, since I was a minister in a children's organization. But my being in church alone on Easter was unusual . . . . As I replayed this information in my mind, I could not conjure up the joy that was almost always present with me. For reasons I could not then understand, the impression became ocean waves hurled against my being—Marvin, go home.*
>
> *Was I uneasy just because Marilee had not come that day? . . .*
>
> *While trying to piece together the puzzle that was my wife, I was interrupted again with Marvin, go home.*
>
> *I managed to squirm uncomfortably through the service. . . .*

When Marvin Horton arrived home with his children, he explains what happened:

> *Usually after getting home I would unlock the back door, retreat, and let the hungry*

children in, but not this day; I gave in to the impression, Marvin, something is very wrong—you go in first.[5]

Upon entering the house he found his wife crumpled at the head of their long table. She had not dozed off; she was nearly dead. She had tried to end her life.

Catherine Marshall relates the story of Art and Nancy De Moss in her book *Something More.* (Art De Moss was the founder of National Liberty Corporation.) There are seven children in the De Moss family.

The week before Labor Day weekend [in 1972], Nancy received a telephone call from her sister Lynne. She and her husband were going on a short trip for the holiday. Would Nancy be willing to keep their baby? . . . Nancy readily agreed.

But this time taking care of Brandon turned out to be difficult. The baby was restless from teething. For two nights the entire household got little sleep. On Sunday Nancy decided to move the baby's crib from the guest room (where it was proving difficult to hear him) to the playroom, down the hall.

While the family was at dinner that evening, Ginny, a good friend of Nancy's sister, dropped in. "I've come to take Brandon home with me," she told the family.

When Nancy protested, Ginny explained, "Lynne had asked me to keep Brandon. I was the one who should have taken him. I just know it. But we had something on for the weekend and I let this loom too large in my mind and turned her down. Ever since I've known that was wrong. . . ."

When Nancy saw that nothing she could say would change Ginny's mind, she agreed and Ginny drove off with the baby.

Later that night, Art and Nancy had been asleep several hours when they were awakened by violent pounding on the door.

"The house is on fire!" The housekeeper's voice was shrill with fear. "Get out! Quick! I've got the children out!"

Art and Nancy stumbled to their feet. The hallway was thick with swirling, acrid smoke. Shouting the children's names, they groped their way to the front door . . . Counting over and over, Nancy at last was reassured—all seven were outside, safe. . . .

*It was one of the children's statements that sent a sudden chill up Nancy's spine: "When I passed the playroom door, Mom, it was **full** of fire right up to the ceiling."*

The playroom! . . . Nancy looked up to the flaming square of window.

"It seems to have started in there," the housekeeper said.

And Brandon—Brandon would have been in the playroom, where no human effort could have reached him.

In telling me the story, Nancy's eyes opened wide at that point. "I still get shaky every time I think, what if Ginny hadn't come—"

I, too, blinked in realization. "It certainly puts a frightening priority on obeying those inner nudges," I commented.

"Yes, it does—except that Ginny said it was more like a distress signal, then after that like an inner shove. She's been pondering for some time now how a person gets God's guidance. In this situation the signal was loud and clear. She was restless that particular Sunday afternoon. Her thoughts kept going to Brandon and her refusal to take him in the first place . . . . Then suddenly Ginny had this strong feeling that she must go and bring

Brandon back to her house . . . . So the baby's life actually hung on Ginny's determination in obeying what she so deeply felt."

As I pondered this story in subsequent days, I remembered how often Jesus had told us that we would be wise men and women to obey His instructions. He even went on to say that when we go through great difficulty . . . we won't be in real danger—if we obey Him.

Yet how difficult it is for most of us to believe that the obedience God asks of us is for our benefit. A story like Nancy's makes it clear that is is not obeying that poses the appalling risk. No wonder Jesus had so much to say about obedience![6]

Nancy Vanderhider has had her sensitivity honed to an unusual degree as a result of much suffering in her life. What Satan meant as evil God turned around and is using for good as she now reaches out to give love and encouragement to others. When I asked her how she knew when God was speaking to her, she analyzed her thoughts very carefully.

The mind is so unique that doctors, scientists, and psychiatrists have difficulty in explaining its total function. We all know that we carry on thought processes within the mind, and if we are honest with ourselves, we know also that we communicate with ourselves within the mind. I may even verbally state a viewpoint and then later use the opposite viewpoint, with its pros and cons, to dispute the very thing I have stated which I had thought out. This is communication with self, and by self.

On other occasions I may think, or verbally express thoughts that I—self—know are wrong. I know, too, that some of the thoughts are not typically of me—self. Is this Satan putting thoughts and ideas into my mind? I rather think so. I base this on knowing self, and I can quite readily tell when thoughts are present that are not typical of my thoughts or actions. Often the terminology is quite different from that which I would use.

Now that I have laid the groundwork I will continue. If I know when thoughts are expressed that are from self, and from an evil force, I can then know when thoughts are from God. Even then, however, I hesitate to say God said thus and so to me, and I usually will not say that unless I know what I heard (the thoughts in my mind) are scripturally correct: that is, does it correspond and agree with the Word (the Bible); does it show love for people, and care for them, and is it appropriate for them? Another question I ask myself is: Does it serve self in any way? God will encourage us, exhort us, guide us, comfort us, and if it is God speaking to us, it will be in these categories.

God often speaks to me through others, and if God is speaking to me through others, I will hear the same message several times, but through people totally unrelated.

God, of course, speaks to me through His Word, and at that time a verse or verses that I have known for years will take on a different light, more in depth, and with an impact that I cannot miss. There was a time when I was searching for Scriptures pertaining to the gift of faith. Everything I read during those months stressed that LOVE is the most important thing to have. God saw to it that I put first things first.

I would say that God most often speaks to me through a thought process within the mind. He will cause me to think of someone *and I will have a distinct impression of a particular need in their life. The need will not always be specific, but rather in an area such as health, finances, suffering, loneliness, depression, and even joy. There are times when God will put a more detailed need in my mind, but it usually comes with a very strong feeling that I am to pray, to call, to write, and always to give love and encouragement, and often this is along with certain thoughts expressed in the Bible. Many times at night I have awakened, not with fear, but with concern, to pray for someone, and this is sometimes for a detailed, specific need. Most often it is to pray that God will put His arms of love around them, protect them, and meet their need. The same thing occurs during the day.*

One of the things I find interesting is that Nancy is often awakened from her sleep and feels the necessity to pray for someone. I believe that it is more than mere coincidence that the Bible tells us God spoke to many of the people whose stories are recorded in the Word while they were asleep, or else He awakened them from sleep. We can point to young Samuel. He came to recognize God's voice after God called to him three times, rousing him from bed. There is a sequel to this amazing account that we may overlook. We are told that Samuel grew, and the Lord was with him, "and did let none of his words fall to the ground."[7]

Matthew Henry, in commenting on this, makes the observation that many people today are like Eli, the priest, who should have recognized the voice of God but didn't.

Such mistakes as these we make oftener than we think of. God calls to us by his Word, and we take it to be only the call of the minister, and answer it accordingly; he calls to

Read again

*to us by his providences, and we look only at
the instruments. His voice cries, and it is but
here and there a man of wisdom that under-
stands it to be his voice. . . . God calls many
by the ministry of the word, and they say, as
Samuel did, "Here am I"; but not looking at
God, nor discerning his voice in the call, the impressions of it are soon lost; they lie down
again, and their convictions come to nothing.*[8]

How like the child Samuel we are prone to
be—unskillful in understanding the voice of God
calling! In so doing we fail to recognize the witness
of the Spirit in our hearts and we deprive ourselves
and others of comfort, help, and blessing.

I must honestly confess that I can look back on my
life and see many lost opportunities when I failed in
having an understanding mind and a hearing heart.
In things both small and large, I know I have
missed hearing God's voice, dismissing it as my
own imagination—or worse, just plain ignoring it.
There have been times, for instance, when God was
reminding me to phone someone, when He was
nudging me to send a card or a letter, and I let Him
down. In letting Him down I deprived someone else
of that which He was willing to extend to them
through me. We need to learn that disregarding
those inner nudges can be costly.

Judy Maxwell, of Quito, Ecuador, describes how
she hears the inner voice from God.

*These do not usually speak of the future, but
are simply words of encouragement, exhorta-
tion, or confirmation of what God is doing or
wishes to do in that person's life. The last time
God gave me a prophecy I was worshiping Him,
not thinking of any other person or situation.
Suddenly He began to distill the words clearly
into my heart. I realized that they were for a*

*friend for whom I often pray. When the pro-
phecy was written down, I checked each sen-
tence against the Scriptures and found that the
message was all based on God's Word, and so I
was at peace about delivering it to my friend.*

Judy recalls four times when she feels the Holy
Spirit has spoken directly to her heart:

*I did not hear an audible voice, but received a
clear impression of what God wanted to say to
me at the time. In each case the impression
was accompanied by peace and a deep inner
conviction that what He had said would come
to pass. In all four cases what God said happened. The first concerned our return to
Ecuador from England, and it was fulfilled ten
years afterwards; the second concerned a
teaching post, which was opened to me the
following day; the third was in connection with
my meeting with Rachel Saint in England,
which took place some days later; and the
fourth was an assurance that I would have
driving lessons before leaving the United States
in the summer of 1978. Provision was made for
the lessons three weeks later.*

A couple on the West Coast became dissatis-
fied with the church they were attending and
prayed daily for God's guidance as to where they
should go. Did God provide that leading? Hear it
from them:

*We had visited a number of churches and
had particularly liked one in the town next to
ours—a body of believers who had withdrawn
from a large denominational church which
was falling away from biblical teaching. They
had formed an independent church body
where they might worship God in word and in
truth. We had been taken to visit this church*

by close friends, and each time we went we felt drawn to the love and friendliness we encountered there. The membership grew very rapidly and soon they had a sanctuary of their own. On their first Sunday in their new church we decided to visit again. Again we were drawn to this body of believers, but we kept thinking we should find a church in our own town.

During the following week, after our morning devotions and prayer, and after my husband left for the office, I stepped into our bedroom, and as I went through the door that clear, inner voice said, Why don't you go back to the church you came out of, and be a light? *I was startled. The "church we had come out of" all the years our children were growing up had been of the same denomination as the one the new church had come out of.*

I gasped, The _____ Church, Lord? *But I heard nothing more.*

Within a day or two, separately, my husband and I came to the conclusion that we should join the church we had been visiting. And we were sure. *During the ensuing week, the pastor of that church called and said that he understood I had been teaching home Bible classes (which was true) and asked if I would be willing to take over a women's Bible class in the church. Very surprised, I said, "I have no theological background or training. I just love the Lord and love His Word, and I have had small home Bible classes just to share with others, but I have never thought of teaching in a church."*

"That's the best kind," he replied; "Will you come?" With those words, coming from the pastor of that church, I simply turned from the phone and said to God, "Since the pastor himself is calling, it must really be of You. So I

am going to take this on the faith that You will teach me through the indwelling Holy Spirit (John 14:26), and through me, as Your vessel, You will teach this class."

And He has taken me every step of the way. I know now what He meant when He said that day, Be a light!

I can confirm that what she is saying is true. The class has grown fourfold. And oh, how God continues to work through her teaching! It came about as a result of obedience to that inner voice.

How can we make sense out of these inward feelings, these nudges, these words which come into our minds unbidden? Does God have anything to say about this in the Bible? Does He promise that we can expect to hear this inner voice? Can we have a heavenly mind about down-to-earth problems?

CHAPTER

8

A Still, Small Voice

God's still, small voice I heard today,
For in the Word I read;
And then when I knelt down to pray,
His Spirit softly said:
"Go forth, my child, in service free,
And as thy days, thy strength
  shall be." —*Author unknown*

CHAPTER 8

WHEN I was a little girl and we had one of our Iowa thunderstorms, I was always very frightened. Mother read the Bible to us, and I remember hearing that the voice of the Lord thundereth. I just knew that was God talking, and it scared me half to death. I now know she was reading from Psalm 29, where David is exhorting his princes to give glory to God and reminds them of the Lord's power.

David says much about the voice of the Lord—about it being powerful and full of majesty, and that it can break the cedars and divide the flames of fire. He says it can shake the wilderness, make animals bring forth their young, and strip bare the forests. David was very aware of the mighty voice of God. You can't read the Psalms without realizing David's awareness of God talking in diverse ways.

A careful study of the Bible reveals that God had different ways of speaking to people. Elijah the prophet had seen God perform some extraordinary feats as he called upon Him to demonstrate His reality. Yet when Elijah was threatened by a woman He ran for his life. Elijah even voiced a suicidal wish! To read that is to feel a kinship to this prophet—our frailty is no different from that of this man, who actually experienced the Lord passing by and saw a great wind shake the mountains, breaking the rocks in pieces. He also experienced an earthquake of major proportions, and a fire. But after all of that, as Elijah stood in the shelter of the cave, he heard a sound of gentle stillness—"a still, small voice."[1] It was the Lord!

We can't outrun God. There is no way we can get away from His outstretched arm, His eyes, or His word. Elijah wasn't the first or the last to make that discovery!

After the awesome demonstration of God's power, one would expect a great, booming voice. Certainly Elijah knew it was exactly what he deserved for his cowardice. But God chose to make

Himself known to His servant in soft whispers, not dreadful sounds. We don't read of Elijah covering his face because of the wind, the earthquake, or the fire, but that "still, small voice" made him cover his face.

I think there is something here for us to notice. In fact, it should make us sit up and take *special* notice: We don't have to be terrified of God; we shouldn't be afraid of that "still, small voice" when it calls to get the attention of our inner man. No, we don't need to be terror-stricken, but we do need to pay attention.

Nancy Vanderhider talked of this "still, small voice" in her reply to my question, "How do you know it's God talking?"

> *I know the Bible says God spoke to Elijah in a " still small voice," but often I am tempted to say, "God, when speaking to me, make it loud and clear, for it seems all too often I can't hear that "still, small voice."*

And my heart echoed "yes" when I read that!"

Unfortunately, the sin nature in man has made him selfish. We have become extraordinarily clever in justifying what we want to do.

The Apostle Paul referred to this in Romans 2:14,15. He shows that we have a God-implanted conscience:

> *For when Gentiles who do not have the Law do instinctively the things of the Law, these, not having the Law, are a law to themselves, in that they show the work of the Law written in their hearts, their conscience bearing witness, and their thoughts alternately accusing or else defending themselves (NASB).*

If pagans who have not had the Law know what is right and wrong, Paul is saying, how much more should we recognize that there is a voice of conscience, an inner moral sense which comes from God.

Dr. David Juroe, a psychologist from California, emphasizes that Hebrews (both ancient and modern) believed and believe that God speaks through conscience. "I would accept that," he states. "His voice is heard when guilt is created after wrongdoing." Haven't you spoken of "a guilty conscience"? Sometimes we say, "His conscience must be weighing on him!"

The Psalms reveal the psalmist's recognition of the powerful voice of the conscience. Especially is this true of the Psalms of David.

I asked my teenage son and his buddy how they knew when God was speaking to them. Interestingly enough, we were sitting at the breakfast table, and each boy immediately pointed to his head. You would have thought they had conspired to answer that way. Neither of them knew, however, that I was going to spring this question on them. When I asked, "What do you mean by pointing at your heads?" Almost in unison they replied, "my conscience." This was very revealing.

When I questioned them further, they agreed that if they polled their friends they would all come up with the same answer.

"I know when God's letting me know I've done something wrong," my son Kraig said. "That old conscience won't keep still."

"You can say that again," his chum chimed in.

We went on to discuss the other ways they recognized God's voice. It was interesting to hear two 18-year-olds talk about hearing God speak. They knew that God got His message across to us through the Bible, through the Holy Spirit, through circumstances, through open and closed doors, and supernaturally through angels, miracles, visions, and dreams.

But it would appear that teenagers put a lot of stock in listening to their conscience, and to them that's God speaking.

The Apostle Paul also refers to the conscience in 1 Corinthians 8:9-13, where he reminds us that we may be a stumbling block to others.

M. Blaine Smith (Knowing God's Will) speaks about this and the strong positive feelings as well as the negative feelings, or "pangs of conscience," regarding certain courses of action. He emphasizes that we should be very cautious in claiming this as the voice of the Spirit of God. "I would not want to say that God never speaks through our intuition or that He never influences our feelings in order to tell us something. To say this would be severely restrictive of God's providence, and the experiences of numerous Christians suggest otherwise. But there is no question in my mind that many Christians today put an unhealthy emphasis on inner guidance."[2]

He is right in warning that we should not look on intuition, hunches, an inspiration, or a "warm feeling" as being an infallible channel of God's speaking. On the other hand, we cannot rule such experiences out. To do so is to question God Himself. Smith points out that the Quaker doctrine of the "inner light," which was especially emphasized by George Fox and some of the early Quakers, was taken to extremes. In more recent years we have seen something similar happen among certain groups of Christians.

We must always remember our fallibility and the possibility of human error. This is not a foolproof channel of guidance, although I have experienced it often enough to know that it is one way God gets our attention.

Emerson said, "A man should learn to detect and watch that gleam of light which flashes across his mind from within . . . . Yet he dismisses such thought without notice because it is his own. Too often we recognize in the genius of another's statement the seed of a thought which we put down as being unremarkable because it came from us." Many people reading this will identify with what Emerson is saying. We hear something said and it sounds vaguely familiar; further recollection reveals that we had the same thought previously.

I can point to at least six ideas for books that have been strongly impressed upon me (I now believe they were of the Lord) which six months to a year later have appeared in some publisher's catalog. I have seen it and had instant recognition: *there's the book I felt needed to be written.* I also know that if we don't listen to God, He will get someone else to do the job.

Perhaps we excuse ourselves because we feel unworthy or incapable. At other times we fail to do what God is telling us to do because we don't set aside the time to do it. Self-discipline is necessary, and a sacrifice of one's time. How easily we become victims of what Charles E. Hummel calls "the tyranny of the urgent"—we let the urgent things crowd out what is really important!

Is there a biblical precedent for what we are saying? We need only look at the life of Jesus. Satan tempted Him to jump off the roof of the temple and even quoted Scripture to Him. Jesus resisted that temptation because He knew Satan was misapplying Scripture. To look at Jesus' life is to see many instances when He was responding to what God was telling Him. You may respond by saying, "But He was God!" The Word tells us:

> So it is evident that it was essential that He be made like His brethren in every respect, in order that He might become a merciful (sympathetic) and faithful High Priest in the things related to God, to make atonement and propitiation for the people's sins. For because He Himself [in His humanity] has suffered in being tempted (tested and tried), He is able

> *(immediately) to run to the cry of (assist, relieve)*
> *those who are being tempted and tested and*
> *tried [and who therefore are being exposed to*
> *suffering] . . . . So then, brethren, consecrated*
> *and set apart for God, who share in the heav-*
> *enly calling, thoughtfully and attentively con-*
> *sider Jesus . . . . Therefore, as the Holy Spirit*
> *says, Today, if you will hear His voice . . . .[3]*

This same passage goes on to list examples of
those who heard God but were rebellious and pro-
voked Him. They did not listen and refused to be
compliant and persuaded.

Actually, the Old Testament provides a running
historical commentary of those who both heard and
responded when God spoke to them, and likewise
those who questioned and refused to believe that it
was God speaking. I have heard mature Christians
advise those seeking to know God's mind, "Put God
to the test," only to have people respond by saying,
"No, I won't tempt the Lord." They are echoing
what King Ahaz said in Isaiah 7:11,12.

How do we gain God's perspective on things? We
come seeking and asking. We pray. There is
nothing quite like prayerful waiting on God. It is
indispensable to a truly effective life of hearing
and obeying God. With that praying must come a
yieldedness, a willingness to be spoken to by God
even if it contradicts what we want to hear.

God knows how to correct us. The people who
lived in Isaiah's time were called by God
"rebellious children" who asked advice from
everyone but God, and then decided to do what He
didn't want them to do (see Isaiah 30). Isaiah's
message is for us as well:

> *For the Lord God . . . says: Only in returning*
> *to me and waiting for me will you be saved: in*
> *quietness and confidence is your strength . . . .*
> *He will surely be gracious to you at the sound*

of your cry. He will answer you. Though he give you the bread of adversity and water of affliction, yet he will be with you to teach you—with your own eyes you will see your Teacher. And if you leave God's paths and go astray, you will hear a Voice behind you say, "No, this is the way; walk here."[4]

God keeps His Word, whether for or (seemingly) against us. The children of Israel learned this, often the hard way. We learn it too, and not always so easily.

Learning is more than knowing; it involves *doing*. One of my children once asked, "Does God walk beside me?" To show a child that God's presence, though not seen, is with us is an awesome and all-important truth. To motivate a child to do and to act accordingly because he believes what he has been told is the goal of those charged with teaching and parenting children. And we as adults are likewise charged with the responsibility of asking and responding in obedience.

Children are often noted for their contrariness. The sobering fact that God keeps His Word must be learned and relearned at many stages in our growth process.

Somehow a good many of us have gotten the mistaken notion that God is in heaven to do man's bidding on earth. Quite the opposite is true: we are here to do the will of God. Though God is in heaven, He has given His Holy Spirit to show us the way.

Writer Jim Johnson comes at this matter of hearing God's voice in a refreshing way:

I know He speaks through the wind and the fire and also the "still, small voice," but don't ask me to articulate how that comes out. I have never had any specific "voices" myself. I've used common sense and said "this seems to be what God would have me do" and I've gone ahead. Sometimes it is wrong. Sometimes

> *it is right. If a man is drowning, and I see him*
> *floundering, I don't wait for God to tell me*
> *what to do. I am not very high on "waiting" for*
> *some signal from God to make the everyday*
> *moves in life that make sense.*

Viggo Olsen (*Finding God's Will and His Personal Plan*) emphasizes that divine guidance is essentially a matter of God applying inner impressions on your mind. He gives you peace of mind when you decide correctly and remain on the track. When you decide wrongly or get off the track, or when it is time for the next step in your program, He withholds or withdraws this peace of mind. The Father's plan is not like a blueprint laid out on a drawing board, with every detail visible at one glance. God's plan for you is like a scroll which reveals His will bit by bit as the scroll is unrolled.[5]

Paul Little (*Affirming the Will of God*) says that if we stop and analyze our attitude, "we would be shocked, for what we are doing is insulting God. We are saying, 'I think I know better than you, God, what will make me happy. I don't trust you. If I let you run my life, you're going to short-change me.' . . ." He continues:

> *So many of us see God as a kind of celestial*
> *Scrooge who peers over the balcony of heaven*
> *trying to find anybody who is enjoying life.*
> *And when he spots a happy person, he yells,*
> *"Now cut that out!" That concept of God*
> *should make us shudder because it's*
> *blasphemous!*[6]

Our need is for transformed thought lives so that our spiritual senses can be fully developed. Our problem is that we are accustomed to acting and reacting as our five senses or reasoning dictates. Herman H. Riffel (*Voice of God*) stresses that spiritual discernment is not a superficial act, but

rather a deep experience of the heart. He points to
1 Corinthians 6:17: "He who is united to the Lord
becomes one spirit with him" (RSV), and to
Romans 8:16: "For his Holy Spirit speaks to us deep
in our hearts, and tells us that we really are God's
children" (TLB).

In Chapter One I mentioned the Apostle Paul as
speaking of inner guidance in 1 Corinthians
2:4,5,9-14:

> *And my speech and my preaching were not*
> *with persuasive words of human wisdom, but*
> *in demonstration of the Spirit and of power,*
> *that your faith should not be in the wisdom of*
> *men but in the power of God . . . . But as it*
> *is written:*
> *"Eye has not seen, nor ear heard,*
> *Nor have entered into the heart of man*
> *The things which God has prepared for*
> *   those who love him."*
> *But God has revealed them to us by His*
> *Spirit. For the Spirit searches all things, yes,*
> *the deep things of God. For what man knows*
> *the things of a man except the spirit of the*
> *man which is in him? Even so no one knows*
> *the things of God except the Spirit of God.*
> *Now we have received, not the spirit of the*
> *world, but the Spirit who is from God, that we*
> *might know the things that have been freely*
> *given to us by God.*
> *These things we also speak, not in words*
> *which man's wisdom teaches but which the*
> *Holy Spirit teaches, comparing spiritual things*
> *with spiritual. But the natural man does not*
> *receive the things of the Spirit of God, for they*
> *are foolishness to him; nor can he know them,*
> *because they are spiritually discerned (NKJB).*

John Mills has made a comparison that is hard to
improve upon: "Knowing the still, small voice of

God is a lot like knowing when you are in love.

"There are many false starts or impressions of love, but when the real thing comes along, all others pale in significance. So also with the still, small voice—there is often confusion and misunderstanding until we experience the real thing. Then we should move on from there, confident that the next time we hear Him, it is in fact God speaking.

"This similarity is no coincidence. It is to the extent that I fall in love with God the Father, and His Son, Jesus, that I truly hear the still, small voice of the Spirit of God deep within my innermost being."

CHAPTER
9

Interpreters Of Love Divine

Oh the comfort, the inexpressible comfort of feeling safe with a person; having neither to weigh thoughts nor measure words but to pour them all out, just as it is, chaff and grain together, knowing that a faithful hand will take and sift them, keeping what is worth keeping, and then with the breath of kindness blow the rest away.
—Marian Evans (George Eliot)

CHAPTER 9

MARTHA Snell Nicholson, the saintly poet who was bedridden for many years, spoke of her friends as "interpreters of love divine."

The Apostle Paul, in speaking of the many kinds of special abilities the Holy Spirit gives to us, said that "to one person the Spirit gives the ability to give wise advice. . . ."[1]

We would all agree that good friends are among the choicest gifts God gives us in this life. They can truly be "interpreters of love divine" who know how to give wise advice.

Dr. David Juroe places emphasis on the way God uses others to speak to us:

> I feel that almost the greatest way He speaks to us today is through people. Man was made a social creature, not to live in isolation. He was made in community to derive help and benefits from others. Thus God uses people to reach others in all manner of ways.

Judy Maxwell gives emphasis to this same point:

> Mature believers with a thorough knowledge of God's Word have often been used by Him to guide me in a situation which I could not analyze objectively. Knowing that they love me and want God's very best for me, I trust Him to speak through them. However, I know that occasionally He tests me, lest I should become dependent on those whom He has used to guide me in the past, by leading me in ways which they do not understand or accept.

Can you think of ways in which you have done something that was contrary to the advice of friends or a family member? Judy is making an important point. There are certainly times when our actions leave others shaking their heads, questioning our judgment, and even displeased with what they interpret as a stubborn insistence on having our own way. And sometimes we *are* acting irresponsibly and should listen to them. But on other occasions we know that what we have chosen to do is the right course of action, and that God has spoken.

I am a strong believer in the fact that much marital failure and many of the divorces we are seeing among Christians today can be traced to disobeying the advice of others, particularly one's parents. It could rightly be called choice and consequences!

Proverbs 12:5,15,18,20,26 contrasts the upright and the wicked and provides guidelines that can help us weigh the counsel of others:

> *The thoughts of the righteous are just, But the counsels of the wicked are deceitful . . . . The way of a fool is right in his own eyes, But a wise man is he who listens to counsel . . . . The tongue of the wise brings healing . . . . Counselors of peace have joy . . . . The righteous is a guide to his neighbor . . . (NASB).*

There is an interesting account in 1 Chronicles 12 which tells of David's friends who came to him at Ziklag. They are called "mighty men who helped him" (v. 1 NASB).

Dr. Bill Bright cautions about making the counsel of others a crutch. He urges that such counsel be prayerfully considered, especially that of mature, dedicated Christians who know the Word of God and are able to relate the proper use of Scripture to our needs.

Most of us at one time or another have heard people quote Scripture to prove a point. We have probably been the recipients of such action. We are well-advised, when counseling others with Scripture, to be sure that we do not lift something out of its context just to prove what *we* think. Rather, the context in which the Scripture is set should be clearly understood and explained. Then, if the Scripture is applicable to that person's situation, we can draw out the interpretation for his or her benefit.

I am grateful for mature Christian friends who do this. It is from counselors like these that we can be helped and can know that God is using them to speak to us.

Dr. Rufus Jones *(If I Were in My Thirties)* provides some solid ground upon which we can stand and ponder. I asked him, "Dr. Jones, how do *you* know when God is speaking?"

First of all, we must get to know God in a very personal way. The only way we can do that is through the revelation that He has given of Himself through His Son, Jesus Christ our Lord. The closer we get to Jesus, and the more we submit our lives to the rule of His kingdom, the more we increase our knowledge of who God is and what it is that He wants us to do and how He would have us do it. Since the Bible is the only book that tells us about God and His Son, Jesus Christ, we must have a thorough knowledge of Scripture.

When we come to the Bible we must do so with the purpose in mind not of trying to prove some theological proposition or supporting some bias that we may have, but rather under the leadership of the Holy Spirit we should seek to read it as objectively as we possibly can and interpret it in the light of the context. In this way we can know what God said to a particular time and culture, and then we are able to delineate from that principles which we can apply to our own situation.

I am constantly coming up against difficult problems for which there does not seem to be one solution. I discover, however, that as I gather as much information as I can about any particular situation and study possible

solutions, then I lay it on the back burner of
my mind and within a day or so it becomes
clarified in my thinking, and I then have a feeling that God has spoken.

However, when we have done all this, we still
must recognize that although we are
regenerated and sanctified by the Holy Spirit
and redeemed through the work of Christ on
the cross, we still bear the marks of the fall
and must assume that there is always the
possibility that we may fail to discern the will
of God. This will keep us from being too
dogmatic and saying "God said" or "The Lord
told me," but rather "This is how I discern the
will of God to be."

I found Rufus Jones' guidelines to be articulated
in similar fashion by others.

Jene Wilson urges that before you go to someone
for counsel, you examine his or her lifestyle. He
suggests that you ask yourself these questions:

Are they living a successful, proven Christian
life? Does their personal, public, and family
life show the practice of godly principles put
into action?

He warns against running to someone who isn't
living up to the proper level of truth "and allowing
them to share their ignorance with us."

Jene also called attention to Paul and Barnabas.

Each of us should have a Barnabas, as Paul
had in the New Testament. Barnabas was an
older, wiser, proven Christian companion with
whom Paul could share his most intimate feelings and thoughts and be confident they would
never be revealed to anyone else but to God
in prayer.

It is really important that we be careful
whom we share with in Christian counsel for

*fear of gossip and for fear of having the very
deepest feelings of our hearts given out to the
general public.*

Jene Wilson says, and I concur, that if you don't
have a Barnabas you should start praying that God
will bring such a person into your life. He also
states, "Your pastor should be the number one person you can go to for counseling. In some cases this
may be impossible. Maybe he doesn't serve in the
role of counselor."

Not only can others offer counsel, but you can
ask them to pray as you outline for them the alternatives in a given situation, or you present problems that need solutions. Many times I will pick up
the phone and say to our "spiritual parents" on the
West Coast, or to our Houston friends, "Please
pray." Sometimes long explanations are not required; we just ask them to hold us up in prayer as
we seek to respond to what God would have us do.
It goes without saying that this is biblical, for we
have been told to pray for one another, and that
the effectual fervent prayer of a righteous man
avails much (James 5:16).

Is it possible to take advantage of one's friends in
seeking counsel and thus jeopardize a friendship?
That possibility exists when we are thankless. The
Apostle Paul demonstrated this when he wrote:

> *Don't worry about anything; instead, pray
> about everything; tell God your needs and
> don't forget to thank him for his answers.*[2]

Ingratitude is a wretched thing. It can demolish a
friendship very quickly. A friend may reach the
point where he (she) thinks he is being used. You
call him for counsel when you have problems, and
ask him to pray. Then you fail to thank him when
the answer comes, nor do you share the answer.
He is left dangling and wondering. You call him

only when you need him; you are not sensitive to his needs. You share only your sorrows, not your joys. What kind of friendship is that?

What about unasked-for counsel, the "advice-meant-for-your-own-good" kind of opinion? The "You haven't asked me, but . . ." counsel. Is it all bad?

If we profess to be living as the Lord would have us live, then that friend who says, "Please believe me, you haven't sought my counsel, but I do feel there is something I must say to you . . ." should be listened to attentively. It may hurt the friend more to say it than it does us to hear it. Such a friend is doing what Ephesians 6:15 says we are to do—"speak the truth in love." Proverbs 27:6 says, "Faithful are the wounds of a friend."

I once had my dearest friend caution me about my makeup. At first it startled me, then it offended me. But the more I pondered what she said, the more I had to admit she was right. I was able to thank her for loving me enough to dare to be honest.

The Proverbs contain rich nuggets to be savored: "A flattering mouth works ruin."[3] "He who hates reproof is stupid."[4] "Listen to counsel and accept discipline, that you may be wise the rest of your days."[5]

It takes some swallowing of pride and a willingness to humble one's self before God and man to admit that we need the counsel of others. Young people stumble in this regard when it comes to accepting the advice of parents and Christians who are more mature in the faith.

But young people are not the only offenders. Husbands and wives fail each other and God when they refuse to accept the well-meant counsel of each other. Many marriages flounder on this point. "All you do is criticize" husbands and wives will say to each other. Can God speak to me through my husband? Yes, He can. The question is not whether God can, but whether I'm willing to listen. We are rebellious, stubborn, and unwise.

Sometimes it's not so much what we say as the way we say it. Here the person offering counsel needs to ask God to provide wisdom and to prepare the heart of the one to whom we feel we must speak. God can shut our mouth as well as open it if we aren't His mouthpiece. We need to be sure in our heart that what we intend to say is what God would have us say.

Our friend (husband, wife, child) might be justified in resenting our counsel if it is aimed at getting even, or cutting someone down to size, or ill-intended in whatever way. There are ways of building a person up without tearing him down in order for him to reconstruct facets of his personality that need help.

A friend's child, in trying to capture a bird for a pet, accidentally killed it. A younger child in the family, upon viewing the dead bird, sorrowfully asked, "Where does the song go?"

Where does the song go when you and I wound someone with bitter words?

When tongue-lashings are our weapon, what happens to another person's song?

How many times have we stabbed others verbally by defending ourselves?

Does what I say take the song away from those whom I least desire to hurt?

Are there others who would know the joys of heaven itself if we spoke more words of kindness and love?

And how many others could dry their tears if words were uttered from our lips to comfort, refresh, and cheer?

The wounds that life inflicts leave scars. Must we add to another person's scar tissue?

Throughout the record of God's written Word (His music to us, as it were), we are reminded that our lives are to be like songs issuing forth an abundance of praise and joy.

Our duties in life can be likened to the notes on a music staff. What discord and unharmonious sounds are often heard because we cause another person's song to die! May God help us to guard our tongues. James 1:26 has a word for us as we think about our tongues: "Anyone who says he is a Christian but doesn't control his sharp tongue is just fooling himself, and his religion isn't worth much" (TLB).

Loneliness is the price we pay for noninvolvement. To look at Jesus' life is to see the God-man committed to caring for others. The Son of God would never cause anyone's song to go! He was the caring Jesus. He was a strong, compelling Person who won the admiration of even hardened fishermen. At the same time Jesus was a compassionate individual whose most attractive quality was that He truly cared. He was never too busy to reach out with the touch of love, to listen to those who came for help. He could not be hurried.

Often in our dialogue with others we leave the impression that we wish they would hurry and get whatever is on their chest off their chest, so we can get on with our own affairs. How tragic! How can we possibly be interpreters of divine love if we are not willing to take the time to share another person's burden? Love for Christ and love for others will always coexist in the person who is seeking to hear the voice of God and be responsive to fellow believers.

Not only should we be available to friends and family members as a communicator for God, but our responsiveness to hearing the voice of God ourselves will compel us to seek ways that we can communicate His love to those who don't know Him.

A word of caution needs to be sounded in regard to seeking the counsel of others. If we are to become responsible individuals, we cannot escape dealing with our own problems. We cannot always be running to others in all our decisions. Sometimes this is done to delay making a decision, or it is done so that if a wrong decision is made we have a scapegoat. Who was it who first made that horrendous blunder?

God called to Adam and asked him, "Who told you that you were naked? Have you eaten from the tree of which I commanded you not to eat?"

And the man said, "The woman whom Thou gavest to be with me, she gave me from the tree, and I ate."[6] Eve in turn blamed the serpent. This was the first case of "passing the buck," refusing to take responsibility for irresponsible decision-making and subsequent disobedience. We have inherited that sinful tendency; but to remember this and to guard against the tendency is to take a giant step on the path of being more open to what God is saying to the inner me. It also makes us more open to what He is willing to say through the counsel of those who are truly interpreters of His love.

Where there is no guidance, the people fall; but in abundance of counselors there is safety.[7]

But what if you get differing advice from two or more sources? And what if you respect the advice of each person whose counsel you have sought? Furthermore, what if the counsel of these friends differs from what you feel God has already said to you?

Do we have a biblical precedent? We can turn to Acts 20 and 21, the story of Paul on his way to Jerusalem. The previous chapter tells us he had "purposed in the Spirit . . . to go to Jerusalem."[8] Chapter 20 sees him speaking to the elders from the Ephesus church and saying, ". . . see, I go bound in the spirit to Jerusalem. . . ."[9] Chapter 21 sets forth the warnings of the Christians in Tyre: "They said to Paul through the Spirit that he should not go up to Jerusalem."[10]

They pleaded with him, weeping (as did the Caesarean Christians) and doing their utmost to dissuade Paul from continuing on. Did he listen? No, he could not be persuaded, and in the end they said, "The will of the Lord be done."[11]

What does all this say to us today? Opinions vary; there are those who maintain that Paul disobeyed the Spirit speaking through these Christians who loved him. Those who hold to this view say that Paul exhibited stubborn self-will and pushed on to the place of needless peril, thereby suffering the loss of his liberty.

There is more general agreement, however, that Paul genuinely believed that his decision was made under the guidance of the Spirit. He was arrested in Jerusalem as predicted. But this gave Paul occasion to speak before the Jews in their national capital; furthermore, it resulted in sending him with the gospel to Rome and the Gentile world.

There are times when we will confer with others, and we will cut across their grain by not heeding their counsel. Elisabeth Elliot was faced with this kind of choice when she, with her young daughter and Rachel Saint, went into the

Ecuadorian jungle to live among the Aucas. The world has since seen what has happened among these Indians.

Sometimes our failure to listen to others will mean heartbreak or unfortunate experiences. We don't always "hear" aright. But even then we can pick up the broken pieces, and out of the disarray in our lives we can work to make good out of bad. It doesn't have to mean that all is lost. The worst failure is not to have learned from failure. God can be counted upon to teach us what we need to learn in such instances when we come to Him and say, "Lord, I guess I goofed; I thought I was hearing You, but I got the wrong message. Forgive me and help me to move on for You."

CHAPTER
10

Open And Closed Doors

*Of all Thy gifts and infinite
  consolings,
I ask but this: in every
  troubled hour
To hear Thy voice through all the
  tumults stealing
And rest serene beneath its
  tranquil power.*
                    —Author unknown

CHAPTER 10

SIR WILLIAM Osler, the brilliant Canadian physician and one of the greatest medical teachers of all time, once said, "Our main business is not to see what lies dimly at a distance, but to do what lies clearly at hand."

Almost everyone at times wishes it were possible to push open the doors into the future so that he could peer at the vista beyond and chart his life more intelligently. But in God's good providence He withholds the key to tomorrow from His children. And how grateful we should be! It is His mercy and love that keeps the future from our knowing.

As you examine God's methods of speaking and His guidance, you note a consistent thread: it was His *prohibitions* as His people (whether in a band of followers or one lone individual) made their way across the biblical landscape. Plainly, it is God who opens and closes doors. Our calling is to continue along the path we are already on, and when we encounter stops, alternate possibilities, or difficulties, we should take it as a hindrance from the Lord, for He controls not only our steps, but also our stops. His prohibitions are meant for our highest good. When you are doubtful as to the next move, submit yourself immediately to the Spirit of God and ask Him to shut every door except the right one.

This poem expresses it eloquently:

> Is there some problem in your life to solve,
>   Some passage seeming full of mystery?
> God knows, who brings the hidden things to light.
>   He keeps the key.
> Is there some door closed by the Father's hand
>   Which widely opened you had hoped to see?
> Trust God and wait—for when He shuts the door
>   He keeps the key.
> Is there some earnest prayer unanswered yet,
>   Or answered NOT as you had thought 'twould be?
> God will make clear His purpose by-and-by.
>   He keeps the key.

Have patience with your God, your patient God,
  All wise, all knowing, no long tarrier He,
And of the door of all thy future life
  He keeps the key.
Unfailing comfort, sweet and blessed rest,
  To know of EVERY door He keeps the key.
That He at last when just HE sees 'tis best,
  Will give it THEE.   Anonymous

From the vantage point of midlife, I now look back and say, "If only I had recognized this great truth sooner! How much anguish I would have spared myself, my family members, and others." Today I am still a struggler (since none of us will ever reach perfection until that glorious day when we are no longer earthbound), but I know I have come a long way. To my children and grandchildren, to those whose path crosses mine, when they are perplexed and overburdened, I now say, "God has a better plan; trust Him and you will see."

It was Job who said, "He knoweth the way that I take."[1] If anyone had cause to question whether God was acting in Job's best interests, it was Job himself. Seated on his bed of ashes, without health, family, possessions, or friends, he could say, "The Lord gave, and the Lord taketh away; blessed be the name of the Lord . . .[2] Though he slay me, yet will I trust in him . . . ."[3]

Hannah Whitehall Smith (*The Christian's Secret of a Happy Life*) quotes someone as stating: " 'Earthly cares are a heavenly discipline.' But they are even something better than discipline—they are God's chariots, sent to take the soul to its high places of triumph.

"They do not look like chariots. They look instead like enemies, sufferings, trials, defeats, misunderstandings, disappointments, unkindness. They look like juggernaut cars of misery and wretchedness, which are only waiting to roll over us and crush us into the earth. But could we see them as they really are, we should recognize them as chariots of triumph in which we may ride to those very heights of victory for which our souls have been longing and praying."[4]

Mary and Martha could not understand Jesus' delay. Why did He not come? Why did their beloved brother Lazarus die?

Abraham could not understand why God should ask that he sacrifice his son Isaac.

Moses could not understand why God kept him 40 years in the wilderness.

Joseph could not understand his brothers' cruelty.

Do you begin to understand that it is not always given to us to understand while we are in the middle of our particular situation?

> *He will silently plan for thee,*
> *Object thou of omniscient care;*
> *God Himself undertakes to be*
> *Thy Pilot through each subtle snare.*
> *He will silently plan for thee,*
> *So certainly, He cannot fail!*
>   *—E. Mary Grimes*[5]

At a very turbulent time in my life, Psalm 43:5 sprang into meaning for me. "Midnight hours" the old-time saints called it, and I experienced it. It appeared that every door had closed tightly in my face, that God was silent, and that He would keep me waiting forever for the answers I so desperately needed to hear.

I was encouraged to read later that this same verse became meaningful to the saintly George Müeller, that man who has come to be known for his great faith. What does that verse say? "Why art thou cast down, O my soul? And why art thou disquieted within me? Hope in God, for I shall yet praise him, who is the health of my countenance, and my God."

Hear it from George Müeller, even as I did many years ago.

"Hope thou in God." *Oh, remember this: There is never a time when we may not hope in God. Whatever our necessities, however great our difficulties, and though to all appearances help is impossible, yet our business is to hope in God, and it will be found that it is not in vain. In the Lord's own time help will come.*

Oh, the hundreds, yea, the thousands of times that I have found it thus within the past seventy years and four months!

When it seemed impossible that help could come, help did come; for God has His own resources. He is not confined. In ten thousand different ways, and at ten thousand different times God may help us.

Our business is to spread our cases before the Lord, in childlike simplicity to pour out all our heart before God, saying,

"I do not deserve that Thou shouldst hear me and answer my requests, but for the sake of my precious Lord Jesus; for His sake answer my prayer, and give me grace quietly to wait till it please Thee to answer my prayer. For I believe Thou wilt do it in Thine own time and way."

How did this man of God, whose orphanages became a haven of rest to thousands of English children, come to the place where he knew he was hearing God's voice? It was through prayer to God, the study of the Word of God, and reflection. Through these he came to a deliberate judgment according to the best of his ability and knowledge. If his mind were then at peace, and continued in peace after two or three more petitions, he proceeded accordingly. Müeller said to first submit your emotions, your intelligence, and your will as best you know how to God's guidance. Then study your circumstances, consult with other godly people, and make a careful, prayerful decision. Then act on that decision, and leave the outcome to God.

Does God have a "closed-door" policy? Dr. Bill Bright cautions that the "closed-door" policy is in error when it seeks God's will through the process of elimination rather than seeking God's best first. He states:

> *Many Christians follow this illogical and unscriptural method with most unsatisfactory and frustrating consequences. Don't misunderstand: God may and often does close doors in the life of every active, Spirit-controlled Christian. This was true in the experience of the Apostle Paul. As recorded in Acts 16:6-11, he was forbidden by the Spirit to go into Bithynia because God wanted him in Macedonia. My reference to "closed-door" policies does not preclude such experiences, but refers to a careless "hit-or-miss" attitude without the careful evaluation of all the issues.*
>
> *This approach is illogical because it allows elements of chance to influence a decision rather than a careful, intelligent evaluation of all the factors involved. It is unscriptural in that it fails to employ the God-given faculties of reason that are controlled by the Holy Spirit.*
>
> *... It should be understood that true faith is established on the basis of fact. Therefore, vital faith in God is emphasized rather than minimized through employing Spirit-controlled reason ... .*
>
> *There are those who assume that a door has been closed simply because of difficulties that have been encountered. Yet, experience has taught and Scripture confirms that God's richest blessings often follow periods of greatest testing. This might include financial*

*needs, loss of health, objection of loved ones,
and criticism of fellow Christians. God's blessing is promised, however, only to those who are
obedient, who keep on trying, who demonstrate their faith in God's faithfulness. The ap-
parent defeat of the Cross was followed by the
victory of the Resurrection.*[6]

That is a tremendously important factor to consider as you face closed doors. Jesus' death on the
cross must surely have seemed like the most tightly
shut door the disciples and followers of Jesus had
ever confronted, but never forget the outcome of
that event!

I asked Dr. Lester Sumrall, well-known missionary
statesman, preacher, and television talk-show host
and teacher, the same question asked of others. He
speaks of open doors and of many things already
covered in this book. But he offers
fresh insights borne out of his own unusual
experiences.

*How does God speak to me? My entire life has
been developed on the principle that when you
wish to know something of a spiritual nature,
and of an eternal nature, immediately you consult the Bible.*

*When we study the voice of God in the Bible
we find, first, that there were counterfeits who
said they had heard from God, but those who
truly knew the voice of God immediately identified those people and said, "You are a false
prophet; you have not heard from God; this is
your own mind."*

*In the Word of God we find over and over
that He communicated audibly with Adam,
Noah, Joseph, Daniel, Ezekiel, and many others.
He showed Joseph his entire life when he was
seventeen years old in a dream. Daniel saw
visions, and through those visions he knew*

the will of God. Ezekiel knew the voice of God from a vision. If we draw aside the curtains of history we see that in every crisis of man the voice of God is heard leading, guiding, directing, and strengthening always.

It was the startling voice of God which brought the man Moses out of the wilderness like a flaming fire to stand in Pharoah's court. It was the voice of God which transformed that lisping man into a veritable prophet of tremendous depth and knowledge of God. When God spoke to Moses, Moses knew what to do and he knew how to do it. And he did it!

Sometimes the voice of God came through others; we can look at the prophets and see how this happened.

You ask, "How does God speak today?" God speaks through His Word. It is amazing to me that even the Lord Jesus Christ met His crisis moments by quoting from the Old Testament. He did this because He realized the strength of God's Word to defeat every lie the devil might bring against a human being. Christ has shown us that God's Word is a buttress and a fortress and a power to protect us in the hour of temptation.

In every crisis in my life, it has been the Word of God that has directed me. I have never tried to use the Bible in any magic way, but God has taken the initiative and spoken to me through and by His Word.

Personally, I have never heard an audible voice that could be heard with natural ears, but I know the will of God inside me so strong that it seems it could tear the inside of a person to pieces.

At the time I went out into the ministry was the first time God identified His will to me. I

had been healed of tuberculosis at the age of seventeen and during that time God spoke to my heart, healing my body and saving my soul. Three weeks from that fateful moment I wanted to go and preach. When I told my father this he told me I would starve if I went, and I could expect no help from him.

To say I was brokenhearted would be putting the matter too mildly; I was crushed. My father's unbending attitude brought not only sorrow, but also struck terror to my heart. I fell beside my bed weeping bitterly, trembling with the fear of disobeying my heavenly Father or my earthly father. While kneeling and praying, the inner voice of divine guidance, which I have come to know intimately through the years, spoke to me and asked me to read Isaiah 41:10,11: "Fear thou not, for I am with thee; be not dismayed, for I am thy God. I will strengthen thee; yea, I will help thee; yea, I will uphold thee with the right hand of my righteousness. Behold, all they that were incensed against thee shall be ashamed and confounded; they shall be as nothing; and they that strive with thee shall perish."

My trembling ceased, and my tears. God identified to me the ministry I was to perform. From that moment I went into country schoolhouses and preached. I heard no voice saying go to this town or that town; but within me, when a door opened I accepted that as the will of God.

Three years later the Lord asked me to be a missionary and to go around the world for Him. I saw a vision of the world going to hell, and after the vision, in a little country schoolhouse in Tennessee, the Lord began to speak to my spirit inside me. I read Luke 4:18.

I had no church to sponsor me, nor had I communicated with any organization or denomination. God had called me and I knew I must go. I sat on the train weeping, and once again God spoke to me within the innermost resources of my heart saying, "Read John 15:16." There I saw, "Ye have not chosen me, but I have chosen you." Something thundered through my being. Within myself I exclaimed, "I haven't chosen God; He has chosen me. I am God's choice, He is responsible . . . ." My weeping was over . . . .

When I want to know the will of the Lord, I get myself quiet, or I will sleep a night or two, and not make a hasty decision. I don't open the Bible and let it fall open (as I have read and heard of some doing). But the Lord brings to mind the chapters and verses. I live this way; I cling to these words from the Lord. When I read something that is a promise, I bring the promise back to the Lord. Know the Word of God, and God will honor it in your life.

If there is one persistent refrain throughout the Psalms, it is the word "wait." God is never early in responding to our needs, but neither is He ever late.

"But," you protest, "I can't wait forever." If you can wait no longer, then move along the path that seems best. If you encounter trouble, stop and consider if this is God's warning. Do not make the mistake, however, of expecting an obstacle-free course. (Remember, you do have an adversary who would hinder you.)

J.I. Packer reminds us that trouble should always be treated as a call to consider one's ways; but trouble is not necessarily a sign of being off-track. God's guidance regularly led His people both in groups and individually through distressing circumstances. You have only to look at the life of the

Apostle Paul to see trouble on a grand scale.
But even if we do make mistakes in judgment,
all is not lost if we are willing to admit that
perhaps we were impatient, or that we followed our own wishes rather than hearing God
aright.

Open and closed doors, God's silences, and
waiting—these are all part of our growth process. Our God is a communicative God, an indwelling Instructor. Remember, the silences of
Jesus were as eloquent as His speaking!

The prophet Zephaniah, as a mouthpiece for
God, declared, "The Lord your God is in the midst
of you, a mighty One . . . and in His love He will
be silent . . . ."[7]

CHAPTER
11

Supernatural Guidance and Intervention

Angels both good and bad have a greater influence on this world than men are generally aware of. We ought to admire the grace of God toward us sinful creatures in that He hath appointed His holy angels to guard us against the mischiefs of wicked spirits who are always intending our hurt both to our bodies and to our souls.

—Increase Mather
(in Angelographia)

Faith come by hearing
now!

(God already healed us, it is our
when we take it; by faith.)
Hear!; my Healing!
come!
Say it!
I got my healing

tell it to keep it (healing)

CHAPTER 11

IN RECENT years some writings have appeared regarding the involvement of angels in the affairs of this world that have set off an alarm among those of us who adhere to the facts as presented in God's Word. Stephen D. Swihart *(Angels in Heaven and Earth)* asks the question, "Are angels on assignment today?" and answers it by citing traditional and biblical teachings regarding angels. What he presents is facts without the fantasies that some currently popular writings allege.

In answering the question of how God speaks to us, we have to come to grips with supernatural guidance and intervention. We know the Bible is not silent concerning angel activity—in fact, references to angels doing God's work appear over 375 times. Furthermore, their appearance may be found in 34 of the Bible's 66 books (in 44 percent of the Old Testament books and in 67 percent of the New Testament books).[1]

And what about the devil and his companion angels and demons? They are mentioned over 300 times in the Bible. In the Gospels alone we read of these evil forces at least 116 times, more frequently than we see the words "love," "gospel," "peace," "repent," or "Spirit." Another 70 references to the devil can be found in the rest of the New Testament. Of the 27 New Testament books, only four do not have references to Satan or demons.[2]

As Christians we are engaged in spiritual warfare: "We do not wrestle against flesh and blood, but against principalities, against powers, against the rulers of the darkness of this age, against spiritual wickedness in the heavenly places."[3]

Anyone at all familiar with the Bible knows that even a donkey refused to move on the road because it saw the angel of the Lord (Numbers 22:22-35). The Lord opened the mouth of the donkey, and it spoke to its rider, Balaam. Imagine a donkey carrying on a conversation with a man!

Then God opened the eyes of Balaam, and he too saw the angel standing in the way. Balaam confessed that he had sinned, and the angel conversed with him.

There can be no question about it: there is much angelic activity going on all around us. It should be comforting to know that heavenly hosts are working on our behalf. Angels protect, strengthen, encourage, guide, instruct, minister to the dying, and provide guardianship.

Many people limit their thinking about angels to the angelic choir which announced Christ's birth, and forget their role on our behalf today. But there it is, in black and white, in Hebrews 1:14: "Are they not all ministering spirits, sent forth to minister for those who will inherit salvation?" (NKJB).

The Bible also speaks of our adversary the devil. We do not have to be ignorant of his ways. The psalmist calls him a destroyer. If he can't destroy our faith in God, he will seek to undermine our trust in the Lord in other ways, or to cause physical harm to come upon us.

There is a warfare going on, and the strategy to defeat the enemy is never to give him a foothold, not so much as a toehold! Where do we learn such strategy? We listen to Jesus talking as He confronts the devil in the desert and in Jerusalem (on the highest ledge of the temple). Satan had been tempting Jesus, but Jesus answered, "You shall not tempt the Lord your God." The Amplified Bible sheds new light on that familiar story. It says that when the devil had ended the complete cycle of temptation, he left Jesus temporarily, until a more opportune and favorable time.[4] The devil doesn't just walk away and leave us alone. He is always seeking ways to bring us down to his level.

Lila Trotman phoned me some years ago from her home near the Navigator headquarters in

Colorado Springs, Colorado. Lila's husband had founded the Navigators. His untimely death in 1956 in an attempt to save a young girl from drowning left Lila a widow who was very sensitive to God speaking. She was also very aware of our adversary the devil.

When Lila heeded the Holy Spirit's nudge and called me, she said, "God impressed so strongly on me that I should call you that I knew I had to obey. May I read 1 Peter 5:8,9 to you?"

Quickly she read, "Be sober, be vigilant; because your adversary the devil, as a roaring lion, walketh about, seeking whom he may devour—whom resist, steadfast in the faith . . . ."

"Helen," she paused, "is anything the matter?"

I had never met Lila Trotman in person. All our contact had been by correspondence as I worked on writing her story to be included in the book: *Cameos: Women Fashioned by God.* During the course of writing that book, my mother died. I was struggling, trying to make the adjustment to life without this one who had always been so close to me. Lila had no way of knowing that my mother had died. "Oh, Lila," I sobbed into the phone. "You can't imagine what your call means to me," and I explained the events of the previous days.

Who could better understand my sorrow at that moment and the longing in my heart than someone like Lila Trotman? Her words spoke immeasurable comfort to my hurting heart.

How does God speak to us? How does He get our attention? Sometimes He uses someone on the telephone! Lila was obedient to the prompting of the Holy Spirit as He spoke to her heart. Because she was obedient, the Holy Spirit as Comforter was enabled to work in *my* heart.

"Helen," Lila continued. "I have something else to say to you that I believe God would have me say. You're going to have many times in the future when you'll need to remember that your enemy is the devil, and he's a trained strategist."

I cannot tell you how often I have recalled those words. Each time the Holy Spirit has moved in response to my cries for help.

The psalmist tells us in Psalm 34:7, "The angel of the Lord encampeth round about them that fear him, and delivereth them." This angel of the Lord, who revealed Himself at different times in the garb of an angel and generally in the form of man, was probably a theophany—a manifestation of God Himself. There are many such references in the Bible, and in each instance the marks of deity are present.

From the beginning of the Bible to its end, angelic activity is seen. Sometimes angels take on a visible form and cannot be distinguished from ordinary human beings. The number of angelic beings is so great that they cannot be counted. But we do well to remember that angels are not omniscient. Only as the omniscient God chooses to reveal future events to them do they know the future. The Book of Daniel reveals them as "watchers" (Daniel 4:13,17,23).

I have often felt that children have the special protection of angels. I can think of many occasions when my own children were small and I felt an angel snatched them from impending danger.

Newspapers in Memphis, Tennessee, carried the story of Billy Baker, an eight-year-old leukemia victim who claimed to have had numerous personal visitations from God during his three-year battle for survival. He died on July 4, 1979, but not before sharing his thoughts on his impending death. "God told me it's just like leaving. He said He's got a room ready for me. I have to leave my family, but they will come up later." He told reporters that God visited him regularly and that he wasn't afraid. The child was able to communicate with his mother with a nod of his head until a few minutes before the end. "Think of the example of real deep faith that Billy left . . .," his mother said. "He taught a lot of people how to have faith and how to be strong. His life certainly was not wasted, and he accomplished far more in eight years than most people do in 80."

Have you ever felt an angel's touch?

The Bible tells of Elijah the prophet running for his life from the wicked Jezebel. He lay down and slept under a juniper tree, "and behold, there was an angel touching him . . . ."[5]

Dr. and Mrs. Jack Van Impe were in a serious automobile accident in Brussels, Belgium, during the fall of 1979. Rexella was thrown from the small car after the impact by a large bus.[6] Someone appeared and threw a blanket over her and cautioned "Don't move her." He spoke perfect English and comforted her. At the moment of the impact and as she felt herself catapulted from the car, Rexella remembers thinking, "This is what it's like to die." After the man disappeared, she felt comforted and knew she would be all right. Both she and Dr. Van Impe are firm in their conviction that it was a ministering angel. The man disappeared as quickly as he had come.

God doesn't always send angels to lift and move us out of the way of impending danger, but we can feel secure that the battles which confront us are not ours but God's. He does supernaturally intervene on our behalf; this is one of His ways of communicating His love to us.

A letter arrived from southern California telling of the harrowing experience of an elderly woman and her daughter.

At 2:00 A.M. last Sunday, April 13, after viewing a Christian talk show, reading her Bible, and praying, my mother heard a noise in the kitchen. "Is that you, Hedy?" she called, but there was no answer. She opened the kitchen door to her back porch and faced a big man. He had broken in through the screen door.

He instantly lashed out and hit her hard on the head, and another hit felled her to the kitchen floor. As she screamed, Hedy ran in and he hit her very hard on the head, fracturing her cheek bone, and another blow that felled her to the floor and also broke the bone in her left hand.

As they lay on the floor, the man ran into the dining room, began pulling out drawers with the intent, of course, to rob. Mom called out, "Jesus! Jesus! Jesus! Help us, Jesus! Send an angel right away to help us!"

The next thing they knew, the man FLEW past them, and out the door! Mom said she didn't even see his feet touch the floor! We praise the Lord that they were not raped, robbed, or killed. I had just been there and cashed Mom's Social Security check, and the money was in a drawer in her desk. But God . . . Praise the wonderful, all-conquering name of Jesus and His angels who help us (Hebrews 1:14).

This woman's mother was ninety-two. Her daughter added, "I praise the Lord that the shock of all this didn't give her a heart attack. When she called me, all she could say was 'Praise the Lord!' How great that she had long ago been taught the power of Jesus' name, and that angels are surrounding us to help us . . . ."

When we are dealing with angels of the Lord, ministering spirits, we are not dealing with tooth fairies or a Disneyland Tinkerbell.

CHAPTER
12

What's The Next Move?

If place I choose or place I shun
My soul is satisfied with none;
But when Thy will directs my way,
'Tis equal joy to go or stay.
                    —Author unknown

CHAPTER 12

WE ARE A nation in transit. Rootless. We are living in changing times. Who needs to be reminded! The world needs illumination and inspiration as never before. We are living in the midst of a society craving for joy, desperately seeking for that which satisfies. We are hungry for encouragement, understanding, and hope. We want direction. And sometimes we need it fast. Decisions.

To move or not to move—that is the question many people have to face. Can God let you know whether you should take that job offer thousands of miles away? How can you be sure that is His place for you and your family?

Direct illumination is what we'd like. Wouldn't it make things simpler, we say! To walk by faith and not by sight or sound is not always easy, but we were never promised it would be. Resting in the Lord carries with it special joys that, in later reflection, reveal the benefits that accrue from having our patience tested and passing the test.

Sometimes the direction our life takes looks absolutely chaotic. Perplexities press. I find Oswald Chambers in *My Utmost For His Highest* daily challenging my thoughts. He says fretting means getting out at elbows mentally or spiritually. We know the Bible says "fret not" and "be not anxious," and we recall only too well the many stories in the Bible relating what happened to those who ran ahead òf God, or didn't really listen to His voice. It's so easy to forget that God is never too early or too late. The psalmist says His ways are perfect.[1]

We don't want to be guilty of letting our subconscious mind project itself as the guidance of God, but how can we distinguish between the two? Is it God or my imagination?

God doesn't argue; He announces. Tozer says we benefit eternally by God's being just what He is.[2] The psalmist said the testimony of the Lord is sure.[3]

Paul said the foundation of God stands sure, having this seal: "The Lord knows those who are His."[4]

Theologians have a word to describe God: He is *immutable*. This means that God never changes in His nature. A.W. Tozer says in *The Knowledge of the Holy:*

> What peace it brings to the Christian's heart to realize that our Heavenly Father never differs from Himself. In coming to Him at any time we need not wonder whether we shall find Him in a receptive mood. He is always receptive to misery and need, as well as to love and faith. He does not keep office hours nor set aside periods when He will see no one. Neither does He change His mind about anything. Today, this moment, He feels toward His creatures, toward babies, toward the sick, the fallen, the sinful, exactly as He did when He sent His only-begotten Son into the world to die for mankind.
>
> God never changes moods or cools off in His affections or loses enthusiasm . . . . God will not compromise and He need not be coaxed. He cannot be persuaded to alter His Word nor talked into answering selfish prayer. In all our efforts to find God, to please Him, to commune with Him, we should remember that all change must be on our part. "I am the Lord, I change not." We have but to meet His clearly stated terms, bring our lives into accord with His revealed will, and His infinite power will become instantly operative toward us in the manner set forth through the gospel in the Scriptures of truth.[5]

Sometimes we would like to be guided by a pillar of cloud by day and of fire by night. God's guidance for the Israelites was indeed very specific in this regard, but would we really want to go back to that kind of leading? Remember, they didn't have the Bible for direction!

That's why knowing who God is becomes such a vital link to discerning His voice. Paul Evans, speaker on "The Haven of Rest" broadcast, offers this word of caution: No one has heard God's voice if what he says disagrees with God's written Word, if it diminishes God's glory, if it attempts to utilize God's power at the cost of His sovereignty, and if it attempts to capitalize on prayer but diminishes the fact that all prayer has as its highest accomplishment a right relationship with God.

When I was a little girl I memorized a prayer that started like this: God is great and God is good . . . . The older I get, the more I realize the truth of that simple childhood prayer. But His goodness is so great, and His greatness is so good; how can I ever measure up? It is a dilemma that throws me back to one thing: faith.

In 1975 we were faced with one of those big decisions that loom as a Grand Canyon of immense proportions. To move or not to move—that was the question. I had heard it said if we are in the wrong place, the right place is vacant. Did I believe it?

Since there was no burning bush, nor sound of a voice like a roaring lion, nor a burning in my bones, nor a blinding light on my road, how could I tell if it was God or just wishful thinking on my part? (And I did wish to move.)

On the other hand, we were torn by the thought of leaving behind friends whom we had come to dearly love in just a year's time, but other factors entered in, and as we carefully weighed everything we found ourselves saying, "God, we are willing to move again."

Two telephone calls were received in close succession within days after we began to pray that way. But there was one glaring problem—the job offers were for *me*. When it came time to make the decision, it was my husband who made it: "We prayed. We told God we were willing to move again. We didn't specify a job for me or a job for you. We just declared our availability and our willingness. This is God speaking."

It takes a big man to view that kind of situation with that kind of perspective. (He had a marvelous job.) But even our son was in agreement. "You go, Mom; we'll stay and put the house up for sale. God has sold houses for us before, you know!" (How well I knew!)

We listed the house and put out a fleece: "God, if You want us to move, then bring a buyer." Some people feel that for Christians "fleecing" should be seen as an abdication of personal responsibility. I have mixed feelings about this. I have used fleecing and experienced some very remarkable answers. Never have I felt I was refusing to carry personal responsibility.

Just what is fleecing? We turn to Judges 6 and see Gideon being approached by an angel of the Lord. The children of Israel found themselves in what Matthew Henry calls "a calamitous condition," and once again needed deliverance, this time from their neighboring Mideonites. The angel told Gideon he was the man of the hour, God's choice to bring about this much-needed delivery. But Gideon didn't feel equal to the task.

Have you ever felt like Gideon? I have. I can fully identify with what he did. He needed to know for sure that he wasn't just seeing and hearing things. Was this really what God expected of him? Did God really mean for him to do this thing? The angel had called him "a mighty man of valor," but Gideon had reservations about himself. He knew he needed God's hand upon him if he was to save the Israelites from their foes. And so he put a fleece of wool on the ground and made his request. "If You are really going to use me to save Israel as You promised, prove it to me this way: I'll put some wool on the threshing floor tonight, and if in the morning the fleece is wet and the ground is dry, I will know You are going to help me!"

Did God respond? It happened just that way! Gideon actually wrung out a whole bowlful of water from the piece of lamb's wool.

Notice what Gideon did next, just to be sure. "Please don't be angry with me, but let me make one more test: this time let the fleece remain dry while the ground around it is wet!"

The next morning the fleece was dry and the ground was covered with dew!

That's *fleecing.*

How do people fleece today? And is it valid?

In our situation we simply prayed and left the selling of the house in God's hands and a competent realtor. We did the thing near at hand—listing it—and then took our own hands off. We have done that every time we have ever contemplated making a physical move that involved selling a home. In effect we were asking God to ratify our decision to move, knowing that if our home didn't sell, the plain facts were that we couldn't move, and we would take this as a sign from the Lord that we were to stay.

The impasses and roadblocks we face, humanly speaking, are as grains of sand to the Lord. They may appear to us to loom as mountains of gigantic proportions. But Romans 8:28 is for real.

Never should fleecing be used for selfish motives, but when we have carefully thought through the decision confronting us and prayed about it, but still have no answer or assurance that we are doing the right thing, I find fleecing—giving God an opportunity to show us circumstantially that we are in His will—to be valid.

Those who say fleecing is not for today point to the New Testament record. After the casting of lots just prior to the day of Pentecost (Acts 1:15-26), there is no further example of this in the New

Testament. Instead, we have been given the Holy Spirit to direct us. That is why we are cautioned against making fleecing a practice. And I would agree that it has certainly been abused even by well-meaning Christians.

We did put our Houston home up for sale. It was a step of faith and a test: we needed to know God's will, for there was much at stake.

What a test! I almost flunked.

The job offer was not something we had initiated. It came as a complete surprise. On January 9, 1976, I hugged and kissed my husband and son goodbye, then walked on the plane without looking back. (I didn't dare! Oh ye of little faith.)

Among other things, I was given the assurance that either I could fly home weekends to be with the two of them, or my husband could come to see me. I was given the finest hotel accommodations, and my expenses were paid.

Since my husband was a school principal, we felt that he should stay in Houston until school was out, in early June. But he felt he should make those intentions known to his schoolboard. Once again, I did not have the necessary faith to urge him to do this. Perhaps it had something to do with the Christian ethic which had surrounded me all my life—wives are to be submissive to their husbands, and it is the husband who does the moving and the wife obediently follows. This was a reversal of roles with which I could not cope.

Within weeks of putting our house on the market, it sold. Amazingly, the house was located in a new tract development and we were surrounded with other new houses (some like ours and selling for less than ours). I could not conceive of someone offering to pay us that much more for ours. But my husband and son with their "batching it" had kept the place spotless.

We found the home in Nashville that fitted our needs and started negotiating to buy it. But one thing loomed in my thinking as an obstacle that seemed insurmountable: we had looked for several months for a suitable school principalship for my husband. We had sent out resumes, had made telephone calls, had taken interviews, and had done all the right things, but still my husband hadn't been offered a job. Now here we were buying a home and my husband was about to resign his fine position in Houston! In the back of my head I kept telling myself, "If he doesn't land a job, then I'll just go back and I'll have to make it right with the company somehow—it's more important for him to have the right job than for me."

But that's not how God works!

My husband's last words to me before he boarded the plane to return to Houston were, "Now I'm going to the schoolboard and tell them I won't be back in the fall. God has the right position here for me." If you were to ask him today if he felt as confident as he sounded at that moment, he would tell you "Yes."

He phoned me the next night to say he had just come from a schoolboard meeting and had handed in his resignation. The effect this had on me was to put me on my knees by the side of the bed for some time!

That same week I received a call at my office. That weekend my husband flew back to Nashville and interviewed for a position. A few days later we were informed that the position was his. To our amazement, the school where he would be principal was three miles from our front door! (He had been driving 34 miles one way over the busy Houston freeways!)

It was my husband who was walking on the water and not looking down. He kept his eyes on God, never doubting. What is faith? It's the substance of things hoped for, the evidence of things not seen. We are also told that without faith it is impossible to please God, for he who comes to God must believe that He is, and that He is a rewarder of those who diligently seek Him.[6]

When faith is weak, prayer should be strong.[7] I did prevail in prayer. That is our recourse; we deny ourselves the comfort we need by failing to offer up strong cries. I shared in Peter's cowardice, but later God was to reassure me that my fears were prompted by not wanting to deprive my husband of that which was in his best interests. I had to say, "Lord, I believe; help thou my unbelief."

What is it that makes us fearful? Why do we doubt? Because we look at the difficulties and forget His promises. Sinking spirits come as a result of staggering faith. If we believed more, we would doubt less. Out of that experience our faith was greatly strengthened.

In our society today we will be seeing more and more of this kind of situation in which both husband and wife need to work. The economics of the times have forced this upon many couples. Some people may take exception to what I have stated, and to the way in which we handled this dilemma in our lives, but we have never doubted that God moved us to Houston for a year to learn some vital lessons and to meet some wonderful people who will be our lifelong friends. Houston was the stepping-stone God used to get us to Nashville, where our roots have had an opportunity to go down.

Houston was where my faith was put to a severe test: Was the Holy Spirit real in my life?

Houston was where we met Nancy—whose incredible faith has been a constant source of inspiration. God has used this dear one to guide me in many situations which I could not analyze objectively. Both Nancy and her parents, who love us and want God's best for us, have been used of God to speak to us many times. Her parents, John and Goldia Mills, longtime Christian booksellers, have pointed my nose in the direction of books that have stimulated my thinking and helped me to hear God's voice.

What's *your* next move? Are you confronted with choices that are difficult to make? Act upon your faith, and you too will see substance. Oswald Chambers says:

> *If you do not cut the moorings, God will have to break them by a storm and send you out. Launch all on God, go out on the great swelling tide of His purpose, and you will get your eyes open. If you believe in Jesus, you are not to spend all your time in the smooth waters just inside the harbor bar, full of delight, but always moored; you have to get out through the harbor bar into the great deeps of God and begin to know for yourself, begin to have spiritual discernment.*
>
> *When you know you should do a thing, and do it, immediately you know more . . . . It is a dangerous thing to refuse to go on knowing . . . .*
>
> *Beware of harking back to what you were once when God wants you to be something you have never been. "If any man will do . . . he shall know."*[8]

Let this be your prayer:

Lord, I am willing to be made willing. When we are totally amenable to the will of God, the divine directive will come speedily:

> *And thine ears shall hear a word behind thee saying, This is the way, walk ye in it. . . . (Isaiah 30:21).*

CHAPTER
13

God Is Both A Listener And A Speaker

Wisdom must sometimes refuse what ignorance may request with the best intentions. Since God's knowledge of our real needs and the way in which they can be satisfied infinitely exceeds our own, His operations will often appear to us far from beneficent and far from wise; then it is our greatest wisdom to give Him our confidence anyway.

—C.S. Lewis[1]

CHAPTER 13

SOMEONE once said to C.S. Lewis that prayer is only someone speaking to himself. Lewis replied, "Very well, suppose it is?" Thinking of Romans 8:26,27, he assumed that if the Holy Spirit enables man to pray, then in a sense God speaks to God. Our prayers are really His prayers. Lewis put this idea into verse and warned readers not to take the last line too seriously.

> They tell me, Lord, that when I seem
>   To be in speech with you,
> Since but one voice is heard, it's all a dream,
>   One talker aping two.
> Sometimes it is, yet not as they
>   Conceive it; Rather I
> Seek in myself the things I hoped to say,
>   But lo! my wells are dry.
> Then seeing me empty, you forsake
>   The listener's role and through
> My dumb lips breathe and into utterance wake
>   The thoughts I never knew.
> And thus you neither need reply
>   Nor can; thus, while we seem
> Two talkers, thou art One forever, and I
>   No dreamer, but thy dream![2]

Prayer is the means by which we take our perplexities to the Father. But do you ever get the feeling that some people have God's listening ear better than you do? I love the letter the little fellow wrote to God in which he admitted he knew God heard prayers, but he wanted to know when God would be listening especially hard to prayers from Troy, New York!

I like to read books now and then just for sheer enjoyment. Such a book is Arnold Prater's *You Can Pray As You Ought*. Dr. Leighton Ford calls it "practical, biblical, up-to-heaven and down-to-earth sharing." Exactly. Prater says, "Save us from riskless rhetoric! . . . God isn't talked into answering by the persuasiveness of our prayers .... If you believe that some people, because they verbalize their prayers so beautifully, have a 'pull' or an 'inside track' with God, then you believe in a God who plays favorites and answers prayer on the basis of the excellence of its presentation .... So who really knows how to pray? ... The only time I am really an expert is when I am praying the Lord's Prayer, for He taught us that and we know it is proper praying .... Thanks to the blessed Holy Spirit, everybody is *equal* before God in prayer. The Spirit helps us in our weaknesses, in our improper understanding, and conveys from our hearts to God's heart what is really there, that which is impossible for us to put into words anyway!"[3]

That *is* what we believe, isn't it? Lewis said it, and Prater said it. You can pick up almost any book on prayer and you'll read the author's version of this thought. God speaks to God about our needs.

One of the problems we encounter in praying is that we are inclined to dictate to God what our preferences are. If we have already made up our minds, we may not hear Him when He speaks! Catherine Marshall in her classic *Adventures in Prayer* speaks of "The Prayer of Relinquishment." She says, "A demanding spirit, with self-will as its rudder, blocks prayer .... Jesus' prayer in the Garden of Gethsemane, I came to see, is the pattern for us. Christ could have avoided the cross .... Christ used His free will to turn the decision over to His Father. The Phillips translation of the Gospels brings Jesus' prayer into special focus: 'Dear Father ... all things are possible to you. Let me not have to drink this cup! Yet it is not what I want but what you want.' "[4] She emphasizes that there is no resignation in the Prayer of Relinquishment. This kind of praying doesn't slam the door on hope. It's called "the pliability of an obedient heart."[5]

Almost every writer who addresses himself to the subject of prayer brings up the subject of George Müeller. His work in establishing orphanages came about and continues to this day as a monument to his faith, and it was all the result of his secret praying. Müeller took as his example none other than Jesus. On his knees he concentrated on talking to God, pouring out his wishes, hopes, dreams, and needs. It was a case of transparent honesty in isolation. What was the result? Catherine Marshall speaks of it as "an inner reservoir of power."[6] You'll find the formula in Matthew 6:6.

We are back to our original thesis: How does God speak to us? Through His Word, through His presence in the Person of the Holy Spirit. Yes, God is a good Listener, but He also speaks!

I asked Rev. Rex Lindquist of Salinas, California, how he understood that God is speaking. He responded by addressing himself to knowing God's will (hearing Him speak) through prayer and the principles laid down for us in the Lord's Prayer and the story that follows that account in the Bible. Hear it from him:

> *Leslie Flynn tells of a woman who received a brochure outlining a fascinating tour of Israel. Even the trip on the 747 jet sounded so exciting that she could hardly sleep that night. Should she spend the money to fulfill her longtime ambition? Was it the will of the Lord?*
>
> *When she awoke the next morning, she glanced at the digital clock at her bedside. Guess what time it was?* **Right!** *Exactly 7:47 a.m. What further evidence of God's will could one ask for?*
>
> *Millions of people search their daily paper to read the columns of Abigail Van Buren and her sister, Ann Landers. Other millions*

religiously study the daily horoscope readings of the signs of the Zodiac and its possible influence on their lives.

It isn't wrong to desire counsel and guidance, but how can we be sure that our SOURCE of help is trustworthy and that our MOTIVATION in the search is sincere?

I would suggest these guidelines from God's Word. One day after the Lord had completed a period of prayer, His disciples asked Him to teach them to pray. They undoubtedly wondered if the Lord could teach them some secrets that would help them to be more effective in discovering the will of God. (How like us they were!) In answer to their request, Jesus gave them an outline for prayer which we today call the Lord's Prayer. Following that, Jesus continued by telling the story of a man who received unexpected company. He was unprepared to feed his guests and went to a neighbor to borrow three loaves of bread. The neighbor protested at being awakened and said he and his family had all retired for the night. But the man was insistent, and finally the neighbor got up and gave the man the three loaves.

After telling the story, the Lord made the application to His disciples by saying, "Ask, and it shall be given you; seek, and ye shall find; knock, and it shall be opened unto you. For everyone that asketh receiveth, and he that seeketh findeth, and to him that knocketh it shall be opened" (Luke 11:9,10).

In these verses we find guaranteed assurance that God will reveal the answer to our sincere cry for help.

If we really want God's will, if we really want to hear Him speak, then we should ASK, SEEK, KNOCK. We must do this EXPECTANTLY, SINCERELY, SUBMISSIVELY.

One can find many examples of men and women who have persevered in prayer. My mind turns to people like Charles Finney, David Brainerd, Brother Lawrence, Rees Howells, John Hyde, Billy Bray, Fenelon, Mary Slessor, John and Charles Wesley, Madam Guyon, and others.

Hannah Whithall Smith maintained that if, in spite of all our efforts to discover the truth, "the divine sense of oughtness" does not seem to come, and our doubts and perplexities about certain matters still persists, even after much praying, then we should wait until the light comes. "But we must wait in faith, and in an attitude of entire surrender, saying a continual 'Yes' to the will of our Lord, let it be what may. If the suggestion is from Him, it will continue and strengthen; if it is not from Him, it will disappear, and we shall almost forget we ever had it."[7] She refers the reader to the Apostle Paul and his rule of reference to doubtful things in Romans 14:22,23.

Jim Elliot in his journal speaks of the "ought" of conscience. "It is important to learn respect and obedience to the 'inner must' if godliness is to be a state of soul . . . . I may no longer depend on pleasant impulses to bring me before the Lord. I must rather respond to principles I know to be right, whether I feel them to be enjoyable or not . . . . This knowledge of God makes me responsible to learn self-control, steadfastness, and so on. Those who are faithful in the fulfillment of this responsibility are in turn promised life without stumbling . . . ."[8] (He refers the reader to 1 Peter 1:1-11.)

George Müeller maintained that continued uncertainty as to one's course is a reason for continued waiting, and that God is often moved to delay that we may be led to pray. The answers to prayer are sometimes deferred so that the natural and carnal spirit may be kept in check and self-will may bow before the will of God.

As E. Stanley Jones sat one day in meditation, the question came to him, "If God would offer to give you one thing, and only one thing, what would you ask?" After a moment's thought he replied,

"Give me a prayerful heart." He thought about that a good deal afterward, and always came to the same conclusion—he could ask nothing better. "For if I have the prayerful heart, all else follows."[9]

There is more to prayer than our speaking; we must learn to *listen* so that we can hear Him. I remember as a child putting my fingers in my ears when I didn't want to hear something. How much we are like that even as adults! Sometimes we don't really want to hear what God is saying, for accountability is then required of us. We are told in Scripture not only that God will listen, that He hears, and that He answers our prayers, but also that we are expected to listen. I have already called your attention to the well-known account of the boy Samuel (1 Samuel 3:1-10), but there are also other similar admonitions. In the Gospel of Mark, Jesus said: "If any man have ears to hear, let him hear . . . . Take heed what ye hear" (Mark 4:23,24).

"Listen to what you hear," He is saying. "You think there is a shortage of my messages? Unplug your ears!"

Perhaps our biggest problem is not that we haven't heard and don't hear; if we will be honest we might have to confess that we aren't always ready to listen!

> Let us then labor for an inward stillness; and an inward healing. That perfect silence where the lips and heart are still, and we no longer entertain our own imperfect thoughts, and vain opinions. But God alone speaks within us, and we sit in singleness of heart that we may know His will in the silence of our spirit; that we may do His will, and do that only (Longfellow).

CHAPTER
14

The God Who Speaks But Is Not Heard

. . . the Shepherd said to Much-Afraid, "When you continue your journey there may be much mist and cloud. Perhaps it may even seem as though everything you have seen here of the High Places was just a dream, or the work of your own imagination. But you have seen REALITY, and the mist which seems to swallow it up is the illusion. Believe steadfastly in what you have seen." —Hannah Hurnard[1]

CHAPTER 14

HOW SIMILAR to Much-Afraid in Hannah Hurnad's classic *Hinds' Feet On High Places* we are inclined to be! I do not find it surprising that this allegory continues to stay on the best-selling list in Christian reading circles, for who among us hasn't identified with poor Much-Afraid and her desire to escape from her Fearing relatives?

Many people, however, never escape the Valley of Humiliation to dwell in the Kingdom of Love. They look at their malformed feet and other imperfections and are overpowered by despair. Overwhelmed by self-pity and fearful forebodings, they do not recognize the Shepherd, the One who speaks but is not heard.

Much-Afraid did escape her Fearing relatives and ventured forth tearful and shaking with fear. But she soon discoverd that the Shepherd heard her cries, and that He implanted the seed of Love into her heart and would make it possible for her to move on to the High Places with "feet like hinds' feet" (Psalm 18:33).

From the mission house on the compound in Palestine (at the foot of Mount Gerizim, where she lived) Hannah Hurnard watched the gazelles bounding up the mountainside, leaping from rock to rock with extraordinary grace and agility. She observed that their motion was an exquisitely beautiful example of exultant and apparently effortless ease in surmounting obstacles. "How deeply we who love the Lord of Love and desire to follow Him long for the power to surmount all the difficulties and tests and conflicts in life in the same exultant and triumphant way," she wrote.[2]

With this as her background, she submitted her thinking processes to the Lord, and the allegory was born. The conversations between Much-Afraid (whose name was ultimately changed to Grace and Glory) and the Shepherd continue throughout the narrative.

As I reread Hannah's book, I once again identified with people I knew. I saw my loved ones
struggling. I saw co-workers, friends, and casual
acquaintances whose conversations I cannot help
overhearing as I ride the elevator in our office
building. I catch fragments of conversations in
restaurants and while shopping. It would appear
that few are exempt from the kind of encounters
that Hannah described. How we struggle in our
valleys! What wretched detours we make through
desolate deserts! Burning deserts behind, we find
endless seas moaning drearily on bleak shores of
loneliness. There is so much that intrudes as we
seek to find our way out of our lonely labyrinth.

Yet a thousand voices seem to clamor for our attention. Daily our senses are barraged with noise.
There is discord in our noisy hearts.

Our days begin with the noisy alarm. If we set
our alarm clocks early enough, some of us have
made the delightful discovery that nature speaks.
But city sounds have all but stilled even this voice
for many of us. Too few of us recognize what the
psalmist was speaking of in Psalm 19:1-4:

> The heavens are telling the glory of God,
>   and the firmament proclaims his handiwork.
> Day to day pours forth speech,
>   and night to night declares knowledge.
> There is no speech, nor are there words;
>   their voice is not heard;
> yet their voice goes out through all the earth,
>   and their words to the end of the world (RSV).

How do we get in touch with God?

We drive to work with our car radios tuned to a
favorite station. But even then we run the risk of
having to hear songs and advertisements which
are an insult to our intelligence.

Rarely can we control the noise level at work,
and sometimes not even in the privacy of our

homes. If it isn't the television, it's the telephone—or one's children, or neighbors, or one's mate. Whatever happened to silence? Even sleep evades us as fatigue overwhelms us and our restless minds go right on thinking. How does one quiet the inner tumult?

Oh how much we need to hear!

Hear, O daughter; consider and incline your ear . . . (Psalm 45:10 RSV).

Is there some secret that you and I have missed in our striving to hear?

Jim Elliot *(The Journals of Jim Elliot)* wrote:

Christ is ever applicable to the situation and needs of His own. Are they tending to lose heart for Himself, becoming distant, carrying on labor for Him without a sense of His sponsorship? Then Ephesus must be reminded that Christ is still central (in the midst) and still in control . . . . Or are they in difficulty, facing prison, tribulation, poverty, and death? Then Smyrna must hear the voice of the Christ who in time reckoned on eternity, knowing that final judgment (God's) would more than right all wrongs . . . .

The plea of Christ in the Gospel is, "If any man have ears to hear, let him hear." In Revelation, "he that hath an ear . . . ." The former in a physical relation speaks to a man who might be passing. The latter supposes a listening attitude in the inner man. The former for conversion; the latter for grasping secrets after conversion.[3]

Let us hear what David in confidence could say:

The secret of the Lord is with them that fear him.

The Amplified Bible rendering of these verses in Psalm 25:14 makes clear what is meant:

The secret [of the sweet, satisfying companionship] of the Lord have they who fear—revere and worship—Him, and He will show them His covenant, and reveal to them its [deep, inner] meaning [see John 7:17;15:15].

Cultivate the deep abiding consciousness of seeing God in everything, and you too will discover the secret that satisfies. Oswald Chambers says that to be haunted by God is to have an effective barricade against all the onslaughts of the enemy. No wonder the Apostle Paul emphasized that our lives are to be hid with Christ in God.[4] Only in this way can we be kept at ease in both the outer and the inner man, listening and hearing what others are so vainly seeking.

It is no coincidence that Hannah Whithall Smith wrote *The Christian's Secret of a Happy Life* in which she shared the secrets she had learned.

In the book *The Life of Reverend David Brainerd* (setting forth extracts from his diary), over and over we read these words: "This morning I spent two hours in secret duties . . . . At night I was exceedingly melted with divine love, and had some feeling sense of the blessedness of the upper world . . . ." "I arose and retired early for secret devotions . . . ." "This morning when I arose I found my heart go forth after God in longing desires of conformity to him, and in secret prayer found myself sweetly quickened . . . . Time appeared but an inch long, and eternity at hand . . . ."

Secret duties, *secret* devotions, *secret* prayer!

The old-time mystics spoke much of this, "secretness," and their writings bear evidence to blessed encounters with the God who speaks.

St. Augustine in his *Confessions* speaks of God as answering when we seek counsel:

Where then did I find Thee, that I might learn Thee, but in Thee above me? Place there is none; (We go backward and forward, and there is no

*place. Everywhere, O Truth, dost Thou give au-
dience to all who ask counsel of Thee, and at
once answerest all, though on manifold matters they ask Thy counsel. Clearly dost Thou
answer, though all do not clearly hear. All consult Thee on what they will, though they hear
not always what they will. He is thy best servant who looks not so much to hear that from
Thee which himself willeth as rather to will
that which from Thee he heareth.*[5]

As Hannah Hurnad comes to the end of her
allegory on Much-Afraid, we see her being given a
new name. The Shepherd asks her what she has
learned on the Precipice of Injury and in the
Forests of Danger and Tribulation as she made her
way to the High Places. She described her learning
experiences as Acceptance-with-Joy and Bearing-
with-Love.

*At last He spoke. "You have learned well,
Grace and Glory. Now I will add one thing
more. It was these lessons which you have
learnt which enabled Me to change you from
limping, crippled Much-Afraid into Grace and
Glory with the hinds' feet. Now you are able to
run, leaping on the mountains and able to
follow Me wherever I go, so that we need never
be parted again.*

*So remember this: as long as you are willing
to be Acceptance-with-Joy and Bearing-in-Love,
you can never again become crippled, and you
will be able to go wherever I lead you. You will
be able to go down into the Valley of the world
to work with Me there, for that is where the evil
and sorrowful and ugly things are which need
to be overcome. Accept and bear and obey the
Law of Love, and nothing will be able to cripple
your hinds' feet or to separate you from Me.*

*This is the secret of the High Places, Grace and
Glory; it is the lovely and perfect law of the
whole universe . . . ."*[6]

God or your imagination? "The Lord revealed to me," "God says," "The Lord said," Yes, we say it, we are meaning it. Sometimes we are mistaken and regarded as being falsely pious: Sometimes such an accusation is rightly leveled for we can come off sounding super pious. How careful we need to be lest we become a stumbling block. We need to make certain that we are listening and hearing, that the Holy Spirit is in us, and that we are receiving his guidance.

F.B. Meyer once wrote:

There is a life in the center of the will of God, so quiet, so at peace with Him, so at rest in His joy, so perfectly content, that the lines in the face are wiped out, the fever gone from the restless eye, and the whole nature still. Rest in the Lord, and wait patiently for Him to use you in helping others from your own experience.

God has many ways of getting our attention. This book has touched upon some of them—dreams, visions, supernatural intervention (angels), friends as counselors and interpreters of love divine, the writings and words of others, family members, circumstances, conscience, the still, small voice, open and closed doors, God's silences, and waiting. Supremely we have seen the consistent emphasis placed on the Word and prayer.

But the voice that surpasses all others is none other than that of the Son of God. We need to hear it again:

God, who at various times and in different ways spoke in time past to the fathers by the prophets, has in these last days spoken to us by His Son . . . . Therefore we must give the more earnest heed to the things we have heard, lest we let them slip.[7]

Notes

Chapter 1
1. R. Dirk Jellema, "He Leadeth Me," in *The Reformed Journal*, Vol. 30, Num. 2, Feb. 1980 (Grand Rapids: Wm. B. Eerdmans).
2. Joseph Bayly et al., *Essays on Guidance* (Downers Grove, Illinois: InterVarsity Press, 1968), preface.

Chapter 2
1. Revelation 1:19 TLB.
2. Acts 16:9.
3. Acts 22:18 TLB.
4. Acts 22:21 TLB.
5. Psalm 119:11.
6. Psalm 119:38.
7. Walter B Knight, *Knight's Illustrations for Today* (Chicago: Moody Press, 1970), p. 214.
8. Bill Bright, *Revolution Now* (San Bernardino, California: Campus Crusade for Christ. Int., 1969), pp. 195-96.
9. Knight, *Illustrations*, p. 217.
10. *Church Service Hymns*, Homer Rodeheaver, compiler, "Trust and Obey" (Wheaton: Hope Publishing Co.), p. 196. ©1921 by D.B. Towner.
11. 2 Timothy 3:16,17 NKJB.
12. Matthew 5:17 NKJB.
13. Jeremiah 30:2.
14. Habakkuk 2:2.
15. Hebrews 1:1,2.

Chapter 3
1. C.S. Lewis, edited by Walter Hooper, *God in the Dock* (Grand Rapids: Wm. B. Eerdmans, 1970), p. 264.
2. The Criswell Study Bible, xvii.
3. Elisabeth Elliot, *A Slow and Certain Light* (Waco, Texas: Word Books, 1973), p. 26.
4. Malcolm Muggeridge, *Jesus Rediscovered*, from the Introduction by Sherwood Wirt (Wheaton: Tyndale House, 1971).

5. Malcolm Muggeridge, *A Twentieth Century Testimony* (Nashville: Thomas Nelson Publishers, 1978).
6. Basil Miller, *John Wesley* (Minneapolis: Bethany Fellowship, Dimension Books, MCMXLIII), p. 123.
7. Ibid., p. 107.
8. Ibid, p. 73.
9. Ibid, p. 114.
10. Hebrews 12:2.

Chapter 4
1. Deuteronomy 5:24 TLB.
2. Matthew 18:3,4 TLB.
3. Matthew 19:14.
4. Matthew 21:16 AMP.
5. Proverbs 22:6.
6. Revelation 3:20.
7. Hannah Hurnard, *The Hearing Heart* (London: The Church's Ministry Among the Jews, sixth ed., 1962), p. 85.
8. © Copyright 1912 by Hall-Mack Co., © Renewed 1940, The Rodeheaver Co., All Rights Reserved. International Copyright secured. Used by permission.
9. Psalm 4:1,3 TLB.
10. Isaiah 1:13,15-17 NASB.
11. Psalm 50:15.
12. Psalm 91:15.
13. Job 22:27.
14. Isaiah 65:24.
15. Arthur T. Pierson, *George Müeller of Bristol* (Old Tappan, New Jersey: Fleming H. Revell Co., n.d.), p. 43.

Chapter 5
1. Hannah Hurnard, *Walking Among The Unseen* (Wheaton, 1977), p. 148.
2. J.I. Packer, *Knowing God* (Downers Grove, Illinois: InterVarsity, 1973), p. 93.
3. George Sweeting, *Discovering the Will of God* (Chicago, 1975), pp. 30-31.
4. Psalm 32:8,9 NASB.

Notes (continued)

5. Extracted from M. Blaine Smith, *Knowing God's Will* (Downers Grove, Illinois: InterVarsity, 1979), pp. 57-59.
6. 1 Kings 3:5.
7. 1 Kings 3:9.
8. 1 Kings 3:10-14.
9. Proverbs 1:7 TLB.
10. Proverbs 4:7,8 TLB.
11. Proverbs 9:10 TLB.
12. Colossians 3:16.
13. 2 Timothy 3:14,15 NKJB.
14. Ephesians 5:15-17 NKJB.
15. Psalm 103:13,14.
16. Job 33:14-16 TLB.
17. Philippians 4:6,7 NKJB.
18. Psalm 37:4,5.
19. Proverbs 3:5,6.
20. Deuteronomy 32:29.
21. Proverbs 19:20 RSV.
22. Proverbs 19:21 NASB.
23. Proverbs 20:27 NASB.
24. Isaiah 26:3.

Chapter 6
1. Alan Redpath, *Getting to Know the Will of God* (Downers Grove, Illinois: InterVarsity Press, 1954), p. 17.
2. 1 Corinthians 14:36 Phillips.
3. Galatians 5:22,25 TLB.
4. Galatians 5:20 TLB.
5. Ephesians 4:3,4 TLB.
6. Galatians 3:14b TLB.
7. Galatians 4:6 TLB.

Chapter 7
1. Acts 22:9 NKJB.
2. *Matthew Henry's Commentary* Vol. VI, p. 1043.
3. Romans 10:17 NKJB.
4. 1 Thessalonians 2:13 NKJB.
5. Marilee Horton, *Dear Mamma, Please Don't Die* (Nashville: Thomas Nelson Publishers, 1979), pp. 13-15.
6. Catherine Marshall, *Something More* (New York: McGraw-Hill Book Co., 1974), pp. 78-81.
7. 1 Samuel 3:19.
8. *Matthew Henry's Commentary* Vol. II, p. 295.

Chapter 8
1. 1 Kings 19:12.
2. M. Blaine Smith, *Knowing God's Will*, p. 79.
3. Hebrews 2:17,18; 3:1,7 AMP.
4. Isaiah 30:15,19-21 TLB.
5. Viggo Olsen, *Finding God's Will and His Personal Plan* (Chicago: Moody Press, 1973), pp. 7, 8.
6. Paul E. Little, *Affirming the Will of God* (Chicago: Moody Press, 1978), pp. 11, 12.

Chapter 9
1. 1 Corinthians 12:8 TLB.
2. Philippians 4:6 NASB.
3. Proverbs 26:28 NASB.
4. Proverbs 12:1 NASB.
5. Proverbs 19:20 NASB.
6. Genesis 3:11,12 NASB.
7. Proverbs 11:14 NASB.
8. Acts 19:21 NKJB.
9. Acts 20:22 NKJB.
10. Acts 21:4 NKJB.
11. Acts 21:14 NKJB.

Chapter 10
1. Job 23:10.
2. Job 1:21.
3. Job 13:15.
4. Hannah Whithall Smith, *Christian's Secret*, p. 227.
5. Mrs. Chas. E. Cowman, *Streams in the Desert* (Grand Rapids: Zondervan Publishing House, 1950), p. 44.
6. Dr. William R. Bright, Campus Crusade for Christ International, letter to Mr. Paul V. Brown, Re: How to Know the Will of God for Your Life According to the "Sound-Mind Principle" of Scripture, ©1963.
7. Zephaniah 3:17 AMP.

Chapter 11
1. Stephen D. Swihart, *Angels in Heaven and Earth* (Plainfield, New Jersey: Logos Internationa, n.d.), Preface v.
2. Ibid.
3. Ephesians 6:12 NKJB.

Notes (continued)

4. Luke 4:13 AMP.
5. 1 Kings 19:5 NASB.
6. Rexella Impe relates this incident in her book, *The Tender Touch* (Nashville: Thomas Nelson Publishers).

Chapter 12

1. Psalm 18:30.
2. A.W. Tozer, *The Knowledge of the Holy* (New York: Harper & Brothers, 1961), p. 100.
3. Psalm 19:7.
4. 2 Timothy 2:19 NKJB.
5. Tozer, *Knowledge,* pp. 60, 61.
6. Hebrews 11:1,6 NKJB.
7. Matthew Henry's Commentary, Vol. V (Old Tappan, New Jersey: Fleming H. Revell Co., n.d.), p. 207.
8. Oswald Chambers, *My Utmost for His Highest* (New York: Dodd, Mead & Co., 1959), p. 160.

Chapter 13

1. Kathryn Ann Lindskoog, *C.S. Lewis: Mere Christian* (Intervarsity Press, 1973), pp. 137, 138.
2. Ibid, p. 139.
3. Arnold Prater, *You Can Pray As You Ought* (Nashville: Thomas Nelson Publishers, 1977), pp. 16-19.
4. Catherine Marshall, *Adventures in Prayer* (Old Tappan, New Jersey: Fleming H. Revell, 1975), pp. 52, 53.
5. Ibid, p. 54.
6. Ibid, p. 66.
7. Hannah Whithall Smith, *Christian's Secret,* p. 102.
8. Elisabeth Elliot, *The Journals of Jim Elliot* (Old Tappan, New Jersey: Fleming H. Revell Co., 1978), pp. 214,215.
9. E. Stanley Jones, *The Way to Power and Poise* (Nashville: Abingdon, Festival Edition, 1978), p. 325.

Chapter 14

1. Hannah Hurnard, *Hinds' Feet on High Places* (London: The Olive Press, 1966), pp. 117, 118.
2. Ibid., Foreword to the Allegory, p. 5.
3. Elisabeth Elliot, *Journals,* pp. 243,244.
4. Colossians 3:3.
5. Translation by E.B. Pusey, *The Confessions of St. Augustine* (New York: Thomas Nelson Publishers, n.d.), p. 247.

6. Hurnard, *Hinds' Feet,* p. 150.
7. Hebrews 1:1,2; 2:1 NKJB.

Bed   What Day to go
tricycle   to Toledo -
Shorts + tops

Ps 105:15
1 Chron 16:22

Mon at East Side Park

frig food -